WASHINGTON INTERNSHIPS

WASHINGTON INTERNSHIPS

How to Get Them and Use Them
to Launch Your Public Policy Career

Deirdre Martinez, Ph.D.

PENN

University of Pennsylvania Press

Philadelphia

Published by University of Pennsylvania Press Philadelphia, Pennsylvania 19104-4112

Printed in the United States of America on acid-free paper

10   9   8   7   6   5   4   3   2   1

A Cataloging-in-Publication record is available from the Library of Congress

ISBN 978-0-8122-2055-1

CONTENTS

WASHINGTON INTERNSHIPS

CHAPTER 1

INTRODUCTION

Washington, D.C., has been called the "internship capital" of the United States, and with 20,000 interns every summer, the name probably fits. More than any other city, Washington welcomes interns with open arms, giving students the opportunity to see how the United States government functions up close and personal. In Congress, media organizations, lobbying offices, and nonprofits, interns open mail and answer phones and run errands but they also write policy briefs, get published, and hear Members of Congress use words they wrote.

Washington is at once a small town whose streets and neighborhoods will quickly become familiar to you and a huge metropolitan area where you can find internships in a vast number of fields. As Director of Penn in Washington at the University of Pennsylvania, I have helped hundreds of students find internships in Washington. Some students know very little about how our government actually works and want to just be there to soak it all in; where better than the front desk of a congressional office? Others have been close observers of D.C. politics and are ready to leap in and join the fray; for these students, a summer at the Republican or Democratic National Committee feels like the center of the world, and in some cases these experiences and the contacts made have led to entry-level political jobs and exciting careers in politics. Other students have very specific ideas about what they want to do; a student a few years ago was particularly interested in Brazil's economy, had spent a semester in Brazil, and had studied Portuguese. Not only was the Brazil U.S. Business Council happy to have him as an intern, when he graduated the following year they eagerly offered him a permanent position.

As in other industries and cities, internships can and often do lead to offers of permanent employment. While not all interns go to Washington with the stated goal of securing full-time work, an internship is certainly the first step on that ladder. In addition to making your resume look good, Washington is an exciting place to be, particularly if you take full advantage of the opportunities available to you. Washington is a place where people come to be heard, and typically these people like an audience, which means speaking events are often open to the public. D.C. is also a natural location for political demonstrations and protests, which are fascinating either as participant or observer. A center of American history and culture, Washington is a popular destination for tourists, the site of numerous national landmarks and monuments, the world's largest museum complex, as well as galleries, universities, cathedrals, performing arts centers, and institutions. So while this book is focused on helping you get the most out of your internship, I also spend a little time encouraging you to get the most out of Washington itself.

This book fills the gap between what students typically know about Washington internships and what you need to know to find the right internship and use it to launch an exciting career. Beginning with an introduction to the major institutions in Washington and types of internships within each, the book guides students through planning, the search process, securing the internship, and using it as a stepping stone to an entry-level job. Along the way the chapters provide advice on a range of issues, from improved communication skills to knowing what to wear. The book offers tips from students, Washington insiders, and internship sponsors, and provides useful internet resources.

WHO CAN USE THIS BOOK

You might think that the typical D.C. intern is a college junior or senior with a political science major. While there certainly are thousands of students that fit that description, not only do interns come from all kinds of majors, but they also include younger and older candidates. I have successfully placed English, communications, history, and other majors in a range of internships where sponsors are looking for strong writers, clear thinkers, and self-starters. As for age/education requirements, they also vary widely and many sponsors are very flexible. High school students are increasingly being offered the opportunity to intern, though those positions are less common and often the work is more likely to be administrative than substantive. College graduates who didn't get around to deciding that they want to work in Washington until later in their academic careers can often start out as a summer intern after they graduate and either use the time (off the clock, of course) to job hunt or endear themselves to their internship sponsor such that they transition to a full-time permanent position.

Whether you don't know the first thing about Washington or you've been reading the *Washington Post* online for the past three years, this book can help you think through the best internship options for you, how to get in the door, and how to take full advantage once you're there.

HOW TO USE THIS BOOK

The book is laid out in a (I hope) fairly logical order; having purchased this book, you've made the decision to focus your internship search on Washington. That's step one. Step two is to get the lay of the land; with so many options available to you, it's necessary to start limiting your search to a few broad categories of D.C. internship sponsors. In Chapter 2, I provide detailed descriptions of employers in various categories, and include lots of comments from students who interned in these places so that you have a very solid sense of not only who these sponsors are (some of whom are also quoted in the chapter), but also what you would be spending your time doing and what you can expect to take away from the experience. Once you've decided for or against internships in the seven sectors laid out in Chapter 2, you're ready for Chapter 3 (and step three), which gets down to finding specific potential sponsors. Resources that you can use to develop your list and important strategic advice are provided in this chapter. At this point, list in hand, you are ready for step four. Chapter 4 is chock full of very Washington-specific advice on preparing the best and most appropriate application materials. This chapter also provides interviewing tips and suggestions from internship sponsors on what they think is most important in a cover letter/resume, and who their ideal intern is. Step five is often overlooked; this includes everything that happens after you get an internship offer. In addition to practical aspects, which include finding a place to stay and making sure your wardrobe is up to the task, you also need to think about what you want to get from your internship experience and then make sure you do everything

it takes to achieve your goals. The remaining chapters help you do
all that, and also help you orient yourself in Washington and include
some ideas on must see/do things in D.C.

WHEN TO USE THIS BOOK

Students often ask me when the best year/summer of college is to
participate in an internship. Policy internships are great for students
between their junior and senior year of college because they have
honed their writing skills, they may have definite ideas about particular issues they want to explore, and they may have some quali-
fications (like courses taken) that are attractive to internship sponsors. But an internship earlier in college and increasingly in high
school can help students gain skills that will make them stronger
internship candidates, which will lead to better internships, higher-
quality work experiences, and stronger contacts with supervisors
and mentors. Another advantage to participating in internships in
high school and after your first year of college is that it provides an
opportunity to rule out some avenues so that by the time you get to
your junior year, you are very clear about what kind of internship
you want to do and where that might lead you. One easy way to
get your foot in the door is to intern in the district office (the local
office where you live, rather than the office in Washington, D.C.) of
your Member of Congress or Senator early in your college career,
perhaps before or after your freshman year or even while you are
in high school. If the timing is right and you're more interested in
politics than policymaking, you could also volunteer for a local congressional campaign. While the work will be largely administrative
(though that may not always be the case), working in a district office
or on a campaign is a great way to get to know staff, familiarize yourself with how that office functions, and maybe even get to know the

Congressperson or Senator. If you still have the policy/politics bug the following year, getting an internship in the Washington office of your Senator or Member of Congress will probably be a sure thing (assuming you've followed all the advice this book provides), and even if after working in the district office or on a campaign you don't think a congressional office or on a political campaign is where you want to be, you will have made some contacts that are likely to be helpful as you apply to other internships in Washington.

As for when in the year interning is best done, the vast majority of interns use their summers to do an internship because they are focused on classes and other on-campus activities during the school year. One alternative to consider is taking a semester off and doing an internship during the academic year. In a city such as Washington, where internship sponsors are faced with a feast or famine depending on the time of year, you may get accepted to a competitive internship program in the fall or spring that would have gone to more qualified candidates in the vastly larger summer intern pool.

Finally, as to when you should start your application process, as the timeline in Chapter 4 makes clear, ideally you will start thinking about your summer internship *the summer before*. A number of the most prestigious internships in Washington have November 1 deadlines, which means you'll have to start collecting your materials and putting applications together in late summer.

Let's turn now to the actual internship sponsors in Washington. The next chapter will help you think about where you want to be and what you want to get out of the Washington experience.

CHAPTER 2

WHO DOES WHAT, AND WHERE, IN WASHINGTON

The centers of all three branches of the U.S. government are in Washington. Also situated in the city are the headquarters for the World Bank, the International Monetary Fund, the Organization of American States, the Inter-American Development Bank, and other national and international institutions, including labor unions and professional associations. With thousands (and thousands) of internships to choose from in Washington, it may be difficult for you to decide how to limit your search. If the idea of working just about anywhere in Washington excites you, bringing your list of potential employers down to a page or two will require some careful decision making. Think of this chapter as focusing in on a Google map; what at first looks like one big place where you want to be is actually easily divided into broad areas, some of which you may find don't really interest you and some of which are exactly what you're looking for. While there are lots of different ways to look at Washington, this chapter identifies seven categories: the House of Representatives, the Senate, the White House, federal agencies, advocacy organizations and think tanks, lobbying firms, and political organizations. For each category the chapter provides an overview of the working environment, the types of jobs that are typical, the people you'll meet, and the type of work that an intern typically does. Once you've read this chapter, you can start to build a list of actual organizations to which you would like to apply; the next chapter will help you there.

INTERNING IN THE HOUSE OF REPRESENTATIVES

GOOD BOOKS AND WEBSITES

The House: The History of the House of Representatives by
    Robert V. Remini (2006)
http://www.house.gov
http://www. washingtonpost.com

Where You'll Be

All official legislative offices are part of the U.S. Capitol complex in the very center of Washington, where the four quadrants of Washington converge, also known as Capitol Hill. There are three House office buildings which contain personal offices for all the members of the House of Representatives, as well as committee offices and hearing rooms. Cannon House Office Building (CHOB) was the first building to be built for Members of Congress in 1907, and sits next to Longworth House Office Building (LHOB) and then Rayburn House Office Building (you guessed it: RHOB). The three buildings are directly across from the U.S. Capitol along Independence Avenue, and are connected to each other, the Capitol, and the Senate by an underground maze of tunnels and trains (and elevators and escalators and more tunnels . . .). Wherever you end up working within the complex, you will likely get to know all the buildings pretty well as you run errands, attend hearings, and scout out the best frozen yogurt.

There are basically two internship options in the House: personal offices and committee offices. The more common (and much easier to get) internship is in the personal office of the Member of Congress in whose district you reside.

Personal offices in the House of Representatives typically have staffs of fifteen or fewer; half are administrative and half are legislative. The physical office space in the House of Representatives is limited; legislative and press staff usually share one room, at best with dividers between desks. Interns may share a table or desk. A rather extreme example is offered by a student who was in a House office last summer: "My experience on the Hill was sharing one cube among three interns. We had one computer, one desk for the three of us. Working the following summer off the Hill I didn't have that experience. I think it has something to do with what they expect out of their interns. On the Hill where I worked where the responsibilities were a little bit lighter, what came with it was a little bit lighter." Workspace can be an issue on the Hill, and some House offices may not organize their internships to provide projects that are more challenging intellectually, though that's certainly not always the case. One student told me about her internship in a congressional office where she spent most of her time conducting research on foreign policy issues, preparing briefing memos and actually briefing the Member of Congress. If you are looking for a more substantive work experience, make sure you ask and get a clear answer during the interview. We'll talk more about how to ask without seeming pushy in the chapter that deals with interviewing.

The other option is to work for a committee. For example, if you have a particular interest in diplomacy, you might want to work for the

Committee on Foreign Affairs (http://foreignaffairs.house.gov). Committee internships are fewer in number and very hard to get; while I have had a few students get accepted to committee internships, I have also heard stories of committee internships being distributed to the sons and daughters of the committee chairman's closest friends. Committee offices are scattered throughout the House office buildings, and the physical space restrictions are similar to personal offices.

What You'll Do

In personal offices, interns are asked to answer phones, sort and sometimes respond to constituent mail, conduct tours of the Capitol for constituents, and may be assigned special projects. For example, interns might conduct research on a new or developing issue area, draft talking points, or be asked to attend and summarize hearings. Before dismissing a congressional internship as too much grunt work, read on.

GRUNT WORK

A grunt, as we all know, is someone who does routine, unglamorous work. Things like making copies or filing fall neatly into that category. While it is true that interns on the Hill will be expected to do a fair amount of grunt work (and we'll talk more about strategies to reduce your grunt workload later), if you are on the Hill to (among other things) learn how things really happen there, a congressional internship is a great way to do that. So, sure, you're answering the phone. But the calls are from constituents calling to express their opinion on some subject ("I want you to tell the Congressman he's an idiot if he doesn't vote for passage of H.R. 123") or inquire as to the Member's views on a topic ("I want to know if my Congresswoman supports this ridiculous proposal to increase my taxes that's being voted on today"). If you are interested in the policy process and the influence of constituents on voting, these are interesting phone calls! You might also be giving tours of the Capitol to constituents visiting Washington. Boring? Only if you think having a special-access pass that you get to flash at Capitol security as you airily escort your party through one of the most important buildings in the country is not really cool. And, as we'll discuss later, being thrilled to do grunt work is just about the best way to land yourself some really interesting projects—like writing talking points for your Member of Congress that you later get to watch her use on the floor of the House. From a student who was in Washington this past summer:

> I think one of the really key things about doing well in a Washington internship is to recognize the culture of Washington and always say yes to assignments and not pestering people but being there. People who are there and diligent at the beginning always get good assignments by the end and the people who annoy their supervisors or aren't as eager or act affronted when they get a menial assignment definitely has repercussions and that person will still be doing coffee and copies in the eighth week of their internship. I think more than other places, there's a culture of Washington that rewards enthusiasm and so by the end you can get really good projects if you show that enthusiasm.

The People You'll Meet

Let's start with the people you'll be working with. First, the internship coordinator role varies from office to office; in some offices the receptionist/staff assistant (the first job on the congressional office career ladder) gets that privilege. Yes, they're just a receptionist, but be careful not to dismiss him or her; having an ally who makes assignment decisions could be very useful. Also, people move very quickly in Washington, with job changes/promotions happening as often as once every year or two. That means you should be nice to everyone and keep in touch with them after you leave, because you never know where they might be and what they might be able to do for you.

Moving up the ladder, an office may have an LC, a legislative correspondent. They are in charge of responding to constituent mail, which means you may well be working with them while you're there. The scheduler is the gatekeeper; that person takes meeting requests, arranges visits with constituents, and prepares a daily schedule for the Member of Congress. The scheduler is frequently putting out fires: shuffling appointments, giving someone the politest brush-off, sending urgent emails to a MIA MOC telling him he's about to miss a vote. If you can do anything for the scheduler, you should; otherwise, stay out of his way.

The chief of staff is in charge of the running of the office; managing staff, budgets, strategizing with the Member, and (on their own time, of course) assisting with campaign fundraising. A letter of recommendation from a chief of staff is very, very valuable, but not if you didn't actually do anything that she noticed. So if you want to cash in, you need to be sure to make a good impression.

On the legislative side, most offices have a legislative director (known as the LD), who manages the legislative staff, tracks legislative floor and committee activity, and may do some long-term strategizing with the Member of Congress to define and achieve legislative priorities. When I was a legislative director I also supervised interns and gave them assignments. Other staff include legislative assistants, who are assigned to particular committees or issues, and a press secretary, whose job is to keep her boss in the news (particularly the local news), so long as the news is good. Press secretaries field lots of calls from the media, schedule press conferences, and write press releases. If your particular interest is media, getting assigned to a press secretary would be a great introduction.

In addition to the people in the office, you never know who you may meet as you staff the front desk or carry out your other duties. Lobbyists, activists, analysts—they all spend lots of time in the front offices of Members of Congress. You never know where a little friendly conversation may lead.

What You'll Get

While interns are not likely to spend a great deal of time directly with the Member of Congress (this came as a surprise to some of the interns I supervised when I was an LD), it is possible in this sort of position to be very close to the day-to-day action. Interns will gain a thorough understanding of the legislative process, the roles of each member of the staff, and the work of a Member of Congress. Internships are also now the first rung in the ladder of congressional employment; having had a congressional internship makes you a strong candidate for an entry-level position in a congressional office.

INTERNING IN THE SENATE

GOOD BOOKS AND WEBSITES

The Most Exclusive Club: A History of the Modern United States Senate by Lewis L. Gould (2006)
http://www.senate.gov
http://thehill.com

Where You'll Be

The Capitol Complex is kind of like a sandwich; on one side you have the House buildings, in the middle is the Capitol itself, and on the other side, running along Constitution Avenue (and a bit to the north), are the Senate Office Buildings. The Russell building, completed in 1908, is nearest the Capitol. The Dirksen Senate Office Building was the second of three office buildings constructed for the United States Senate. Located northeast of the Capitol on a site bounded by Constitution Avenue, C Street, First Street, and Second Street N.E., it adjoins the more modern looking Hart Senate Office Building. Like most things about the Senate, the buildings on the Senate side are more glamorous and grand than the House buildings. Remember that in the House, each of the 435 Members represents a little over 600,000 people; in the Senate, most of the 100 Senators represent millions each. While there are states with populations the size of a congressional district (North Dakota, Vermont, Delaware), think of states the size of California (population 36 million) or Texas (23 million). As a result, offices in the Senate are larger than in the House, with staffs of as many as forty, depending on the size of their staffing budget, which is based on the population of the state the Senator represents.

During the summer, a Senate office will generally have three to seven interns, though some offices find room for as many as ten, and often they run two six-week sessions to give more students the opportunity to intern. The physical size of the office, which dictates how many staff and interns a Senator can house, depends somewhat on the Senator's seniority, which building she is in, and the population of the State they represent. Offices in Russell are smaller than those in Hart or Dirksen and may be divided among several floors.

As in the House, you are most likely to find an internship with one of the two Senators from your home state, though committee offices are always worth a try. Also look at the websites for the leadership offices; there are very few internship positions available in these but it can't hurt to ask.

What You'll Do

All interns will be expected to help the staff assistants in answering phones, sorting and sometimes responding to constituent mail, and conducting tours of the Capitol for constituents. As an example of the funny things interns are sometimes asked to do, you might be asked to save a field on the National Mall (the national park area that runs from the Congress, past the White House, up to the Lincoln Memorial) for office softball games. If an intern is particularly interested in press issues, he may become the special intern of the press office. This person will be expected to arrive around 7:30 A.M. to search for articles that mention the Senator and send out a staff email. Occasionally, a legislative assistant might ask an intern to conduct research on a new or developing issue area, draft talking points, or attend hearings. Depending on the office, there may be special projects that interns work on over the course of the internship. Liz Conroy describes the intern project in Senator Bob Casey's office:

> Interns who get to know and really work well with their legislative mentors can bring new ideas to the table. We ask our interns over the course of their internship to come up with a bill and what we really said was, this is not just a chance for you to come out of this internship with a writing sample, which is always good, but if there's a great idea you come up with we will work with you to see if that's something our office can do. As a freshman office we are constantly looking to define ourselves and figure out unique ways for the Senator to get involved in issues and prioritize his agenda and sometimes unique ideas from interns get the ball rolling.

The People You'll Meet

Like the House, there are pretty clear divisions between people who keep the office running smoothly and handle the more political end of things (the chief of staff, schedulers, front office staff) and legislative staff (i.e., legislative assistants and the director). You'll also have staff handling constituent concerns (i.e., legislative correspondents) and the press office. What these people do is mostly similar to what people do on the House side, just bigger. There are more staff doing these jobs, there are more constituents, more issues, more visitors—you get the idea. Also, probably because there are more staff to go around, staff on the Senate side are more likely to be specialists. On the House side, you'll typically have three legislative assistants; Members typically get two committee assignments, so two of those LAs will get a committee each, plus a few other issues to cover when they come to the full House for votes. The third LA covers everything that's left. On the Senate side, you'll have multiple staff assigned to each committee, and because of the more demanding schedule a Senator has, staff tend to do much more of the legwork before the Senator gets involved.

What You'll Get

As in the House, interns will likely gain a thorough understanding of the roles of each member of the staff and the busy life of a Senator. Liz Conroy in Senator Casey's office describes the ebb and flow of a summer internship on the Senate side: "Summer is great because there's a mix of recess time and heavy in-session time so they get to see everything from the drive and subsequent release when we finally get to recess. They'll see heavy mail and call in campaigns from interest groups and so they get to see how advocacy works from inside a Senate office and then in recess they get more time to work on their own projects."

Also as in the House, many senior staff started as interns. This means you're gaining valuable experience and it also suggests that staff are likely to see you as a potential hire in the future. You may get some great writing samples that you can use for your next application; we'll talk later about the writing skills that you'll probably acquire. You'll also get to be in the Senate, surrounded by some of the most powerful people in the world. If you're any kind of policy junkie, this is exciting stuff. One student shared her impressions of being on the Senate side: "It was just an incredible experience to be in the Senate. From the outside, it's hard to understand how the process works—it seems like nothing ever gets accomplished but when you work there you understand why the process is so slow and you learn how the process was designed to take a long time for things to change. You get a great understanding of how government really works and you also get to see Senators working down the hall so it was a really memorable experience."

INTERNING AT THE WHITE HOUSE

GOOD BOOKS, ARTICLES, AND WEBSITES

The Modern Presidency by James P. Pfiffner (2007)
The Executive Office of the President: A Historical, Biographical, and Bibliographical Guide edited by Harold C. Relyea; published in cooperation with the Center for the Study of the Presidency (1997)
Articles in *Presidential Studies Quarterly*
http://www.whitehouse.gov

Where You'll Be

Arriving at the White House complex each morning will likely give you a bit of a thrill every day of your internship. Once you are through the gates, however, it is important that your expectations are based on reality. If you are accepted to intern at the White House, do not expect to be placed in the West Wing. The White House accepts 100 interns each summer, the majority of whom work in the Old Executive Office Building, part of the White House complex but not part of the White House itself. Almost half of the White House interns are assigned to the Correspondence office, which is practically run by interns. See the box for other possible assignments.

WHITE HOUSE OFFICES: INTERNSHIP SPONSORS

(http://www.whitehouse.gov/government/off-descrp.html)

Advance: coordinates all logistical arrangements for presidential visits.

Cabinet Liaison: primary point of contact for Cabinet members and agency heads.

White House Counsel: advises the President on all legal issues.

Communications: responsible for the President's media events.

Correspondence: processes all correspondence addressed to the President.

Domestic Policy Council: coordinates the domestic policy-making process.

Fellows: oversees White House Fellows program.

Intergovernmental Affairs: liaison to state, local, and tribal governments.

Legislative Affairs: liaison to the United States Congress.

First Lady's office: coordinates and schedules events involving the First Lady.

National Economic Council: advises President on U.S. and
global economic policy.

Office of the Vice President: assists Vice President in his
executive and legislative duties.

Political Affairs: "ensures that the executive branch and the
President are aware of the concerns of the American citizen."
(This office was started under President Reagan and has
been involved in partisan activities. I'm not sure how they get
away with being political on the public's dime but they do.)

Public Liaison: plans briefings, meetings, and large events.

Photo Office: photographically documents and maintains an
archive.

Presidential Personnel: recruits, screens, and recommends
qualified candidates for Presidential appointments to federal
departments and agencies.

Scheduling: plans and implements the President's daily and
long-range schedules. Speechwriting: crafts the President's
formal speeches and other remarks.

Strategic Initiatives: plans and implements strategy for achieving
Presidential priorities.

Travel Office: provides logistical travel support.

White House Management: manages the daily operations.

White House Personnel: manages staff employment and runs
the intern program.

What You'll Do

Depending on your assignment, you may be making copies,
answering phones, helping tourists, or responding to mail. As in
most internships in D.C., if you are willing to complete these mundane tasks with alacrity and good humor, you may be assigned more
interesting projects. There is an online application but be warned:

students who apply to the White House often don't hear if they're accepted until very late. For summer, it isn't uncommon to hear back from their hiring office in April. We'll talk more about your application strategy in the next chapter.

The People You'll Meet

Because of the size of the White House complex and the variety of the offices where you might be placed, the people you meet will vary widely. For example, if you are in the press office you will likely meet the various members of the press team, and you may communicate with reporters and other members of the media. When you choose your preferred office assignments, you might think about the people who work in and with that office and if they are in a field that might be helpful to you for your next internship or job.

What You'll Get

In addition to normal office duties, interns attend weekly lectures, volunteer at special events, participate in tours, and contribute to a community service project in the Washington, D.C., area. If you have a successful experience, you'll also walk away with email addresses for at least two or three people who are willing to speak to your skills as a reference. Regardless, a White House internship is very prestigious, and just having that on your resume will help you obtain future internships and jobs in Washington.

INTERNING IN A FEDERAL AGENCY

GOOD BOOKS AND WEBSITES

System Under Stress: Homeland Security and American Politics
by Donald F. Kettl (2007)

The New Public Service: Serving, Not Steering by Janet Vinzant
Denhardt and Robert B. Denhardt (2007)
http://www.usa.gov/Agencies/Federal/All_Agencies/index.
shtml

Where You'll Be

In addition to the White House, the executive branch of the federal government includes departments, agencies, government corporations, boards, commissions, and committees. The website in the box at the top of this page is worth a browse to get a sense of the vast numbers of offices that make up the federal government. Many of these are located near the Capitol or the White House and along the mall, but others are scattered around Washington and in the suburbs and beyond. Each of these bodies is extremely specialized and has very different organizational structures. Interning in one of these offices could be one way to get very close to the day-to-day functioning of the government.

INTERNING FOR THE FEDS

Federal Bureau of Investigation

https://www.fbijobs.gov/honors.asp

From their website: "Once selected, FBI Interns can look forward to three extremely rewarding and interesting months. You'll be working side-by-side with Special Agents and Professional Support personnel on important cases and procedures. You'll feel like you're a part of the Bureau . . . because you are. Upon arriving in Washington, D.C., Honors Interns will attend an orientation at the FBI Headquarters. Interns will be assigned to an FBI Headquarters division based on their academic discipline, potential contribution to the division, and the needs of the FBI. For instance, interns whose discipline is in the physical sciences may be assigned to the FBI Laboratory's Forensic Science Research and Training Center in nearby Quantico, Virginia. All interns will be under the Supervision of the Assistant Director of their assigned division. By the end of your internship, you will have a thorough understanding of the inner workings of the FBI." FBI interns are paid at the GS-6 level, which works out to about $2,000 a month. Deadline is November 1.

Central Intelligence Agency

http://www.cia.gov/emplooyment/student.html1#top

From their website: "You will be given the opportunity to work with highly-skilled professionals and see first-hand the role the CIA plays in supporting US officials who make our country's foreign policy. We are interested in students majoring in engineering, computer science, mathematics, economics, physical sciences, foreign languages, area studies, business administration, accounting, international relations, finance, logistics, human resources, geography, national security studies, military and foreign affairs, political science and graphic design. Interns are required to work either a combination of one semester and one summer internship, or two 90-day summer internships." CIA pay is competitive, and their deadline is November 1.

United States Department of State

http://www.careers.state.gov/student/programs/student_internships.html

From their website: "It's an opportunity for you to get an inside look at the different types of positions and responsibilities available in foreign affairs. Think of it as taking a career test ride before you actually have to decide what you are going to do with your life." Students tentatively selected for the internship program must undergo a background investigation and receive either a secret or top secret security clearance. Deadline is November 1.

What You'll Do

Because of the huge variety of placements possible, it's very hard to say what you might do. One student at the Federal Trade Commission this past summer spent most of his time working on legal briefs, which was great preparation for law school. Another student with the Special Inspector General for Iraq Reconstruction spent much of her time researching and writing for a book the office was preparing on the story of Iraq reconstruction. Another student at the Department of Defense spent most of his time finding his way around the Pentagon and running errands. As we'll discuss in the next chapter, it is critical that you ask questions during the interview so that you're clear on what kind of assignments you can expect. We'll also talk more about strategies to get better assignments.

THE FEDERAL GOVERNMENT WANTS YOU ... WE THINK ...

According to Call to Serve, a nonprofit whose mission is to encourage young people to seek jobs with the federal government, the federal government will need to fill 193,000 "mission-critical" positions by 2009. You might think that given their need to recruit high-quality personnel there would be countless internship opportunities available. Unfortunately, it is not easy to find open internship positions, and the hiring process is often tedious. There are two websites that might be helpful: http://studentjobs.gov and http://www.makingthedifference.org/index.shtml.

As for timing, while it's possible to find an announcement for an internship at one of the agencies in March for the coming summer, there are a number of federal agencies that require a very early start. For these agencies, they often suggest you start collecting the required documents a full year before the summer you intend to participate in the internship, and their deadline for applications is typically November for a June start date. While the more competitive and prestigious internships do tend to have earlier deadlines, the other practical reason for the early deadline is that applicants have to go through a security clearance process. More on security clearance in the next chapter.

The People You'll Meet

This of course varies widely depending on your assignment and your networking skills. One student who was assigned directly to an Assistant Secretary at the Department of Commerce spent all of her time working closely with senior staff and came away with a solid understanding of the work of the office and lots of good contacts. Another student at the Department of Health and Human Services was assigned generally to an office and really never got past answering phones, so was not able to connect with staff in a way that showed off his research skills. Again, it's best to be clear in the interview what the workload will be and how you will be assigned work so that you can make an informed decision about the internship offer.

What You'll Get

Federal agencies often use internships as a way to recruit individuals for full-time work, so choosing an internship in an issue area that is of particular interest to you could well lead to employment after college or at the very least some well-placed references.

INTERNING IN AN ADVOCACY ORGANIZATION
OR THINK TANK

GOOD BOOKS

Interest Group Politics by Allan J. Cigler and Burdett A. Loomis
(2006)

"Advocacy Organizations in the U.S. Political Process" by K. T.
Andrews and B. Edwards, *Annual Review of Sociology* 30:
479-506 (2004)

In this section we'll talk about two similar types of organizations: advocacy groups and think tanks. Advocacy groups are nonprofit organizations that run the gamut from tiny to impressively large. Unlike think tanks, advocacy groups don't typically have lots of Ph.D.s on staff who write big books and spend their Sunday mornings on television (though some do). Advocacy groups are perhaps a little more connected to issue campaigns on which their organization takes a position and conducts, well, advocacy to achieve their goals. This might include getting the word out to their members, who then contact their Members of Congress; meeting directly with Members of Congress or providing congressional testimony; and holding events that might get picked up by the media. For example, Common Cause is a very old and well-respected organization that sees itself as a "vehicle for citizens to make their voices heard in the political process and to hold their elected leaders accountable to the public interest." That means they take an issue—say, for example, money in politics—and conduct some research, talk to people, and then try to change how things are done. In the money in politics example, they spend a lot of time trying to change campaign finance law so that wealthy people don't have more influence in politics than everyone else, which is their view of the status quo.

The profile for think tanks is a little different, though sometimes the differences are not terribly clear. Like some of the most well-established advocacy organizations, there are a number of think tanks in Washington that are very well funded and have large staffs. While the work varies widely, at think tanks the work is more focused on research and on informing policy debate, rather than directly influencing policy debates. This is not to say that they don't have a clear political view; almost all of them have a consistent political perspective on policy issues and most are fairly open about where they fall on the political spectrum. To get a better sense of what think tanks do, see the profiles that follow.

American Enterprise Institute

http://www.aei.org

AEI is a conservative think tank, founded in 1943. It is associated with neoconservative domestic and foreign policy views. According to the institute its mission is "to defend the principles and improve the institutions of American freedom and democratic capitalism—limited government, private enterprise, individual liberty and responsibility, vigilant and effective defense and foreign policies, political accountability, and open debate."

AEI has a large internship program, accepting fifty students each spring, summer, and fall. The work is substantive, and students are assigned to an issue area that matches their interests (economic policy, foreign and defense studies, social and political studies, media affairs, *The American* magazine, publications editing, information systems, marketing, and human resources). Interns are also assigned a policy mentor in their area of interest. Internships are unpaid, but AEI interns don't have to worry about a food budget; AEI interns enjoy a complimentary gourmet breakfast and lunch. AEI also arranges a number of lectures and discussions with impressive speakers and coordinates a number of tours for each of their intern classes.

Center for American Progress

http://www.americanprogress.org

On the opposite side of the political spectrum you will find CAP, which was started in 2003 by John Podesta, former chief of staff to President Clinton. CAP's stated mission is to create a "long-term, progressive vision for America—a vision that policy makers, thought-leaders and activists can use to shape the national debate and pass laws that make a difference." Their staff and fellows work on a wide range of policy issues, organizing events, producing reports, and providing congressional testimony.

With a staff of 150, CAP brings in fifty interns each term to work on one of their issue teams. Interns participate in meetings, contribute to research projects, and are invited to discussions with organizational leadership. The program provides a stipend, but no gourmet lunch.

Where You'll Be

There is a vast range of nonprofit advocacy organizations in Washington representing particular interests. On one end of the spectrum are small organizations working on a single issue and with very limited budgets and hence staffing. EPIC, the Education for Peace in Iraq Center, has two rooms above a shop on Capitol Hill. There are thousands of organizations like EPIC working on campaign finance, gun control, the death penalty, you name it. Their staffs might be limited to a founder and an assistant, or may be a little bigger as a result of a successful grant application. On the other end of the spectrum are multi-issue flagship organizations that have been around for decades, are highly visible, and have strong fundraising capability. They may have staffs of a hundred or more and can afford to recruit academics and others from the top of their respective fields. These think tanks and advocacy and membership organizations often own impressive real estate scattered across Washington, where their names are proudly displayed above the front door. Organizations such as these (Brookings Institution, Cato, the Children's Defense Fund, the Heritage Foundation, AARP...) typically have large, organized internship programs that sponsor a dozen or more interns every summer.

What You'll Do

Many of the smaller organizations have limited resources, which means they usually don't have enough staff to do everything they would like to do, and are not able to pay high salaries to the staff they have. This has several consequences. First, these employers tend to have a staff that is committed to the organization's cause. Second, staff are given freedom to take on new projects, which can be an opportunity to establish themselves as an authority on an issue. Third, interns are welcome and are often provided the opportunity to contribute meaningfully to the work of the organization. An intern working for an advocacy organization may be asked to prepare reports or fact sheets that the organization will publish, to write congressional testimony, or to conduct research on a new issue area. Working for EPIC, for example, you might write for their blog, conduct research, and help publicize their programs.

In the larger organizations, you will typically be assigned to an office that is either administrative or focused on a policy area. At the Children's Defense Fund, for example, you can ask to be assigned to the President's office, which will provide great exposure to nonprofit management. You might instead choose an assignment with its health or juvenile justice divisions, where your work will likely be more directly related to policy-making.

At a think tank, you may be assigned to a particular scholar whose area of expertise matches your area of interest or you may find yourself working for the editor of their journal. You are likely to spend some time completing administrative tasks, and you may also be asked to write short articles or one-pagers that are posted to their website or published in their journal, perhaps even coauthoring a research article with a scholar whose work you admire.

The People You'll Meet

These groups frequently work in coalition with one another and often socialize together. As on the Hill there are opportunities to attend briefings, receptions, and lunch events. You may work with top names in your field if you are working for one of the better-known groups. Even if you're working in a smaller organization, opportunities to meet interesting people should abound.

What You'll Get

This is an excellent choice for a student who wants to work on a particular issue area, such as children's health, foreign policy, or minority issues. This sort of internship experience could lead to full-time work with an advocacy organization. While many individuals continue their work in advocacy organizations, others use their advocacy experience to move into positions in Congress or in one of the federal agencies. My experience is an excellent example. Early in my career, I was a policy analyst at National Council of La Raza, the nation's largest Hispanic advocacy organization. While my focus was poverty policy, I was particularly interested in employment policy, and since NCLR didn't have an employment project at the time, I was able to add that to my area of expertise. As a result I was part of NCLR's advocacy campaign on the issue of worker retraining needs during congressional consideration of the North American Free Trade Agreement (NAFTA). I made an impression on Congressman Becerra's legislative assistant, with whom I met to discuss NCLR's position on NAFTA, and when he decided to go back to graduate school, he suggested I consider becoming Congressman Becerra's legislative assistant for education and labor. I was offered the position and within two years I was Congressman Becerra's legislative director. This trajectory is not uncommon in Washington, where people change jobs within two years and there's always a more interesting job around the corner.

As for the pros and cons of working in a large think tank versus a small advocacy organization, two students who were in small advocacy organizations last summer had this to say:

In the smaller places, I feel like you get a more personal experience. In my office there were as many interns as there were staff and that created a culture where the interns and staff were good friends. If you talk to them and also find out what they're interested in, then you can really have a great experience because you can really engage them (college senior).

My office was small so it really was like we were members of the staff. I think the good thing about a small office is you can work with everyone. We did research, we did event planning; even if there were some aspects that I don't think I would want to do in the future I'm glad I got a chance to do some of these things even if only just to rule them out (college junior).

INTERNING IN A LOBBYING FIRM

GOOD BOOKS AND WEBSITES

Total Lobbying: What Lobbyists Want (and How They Try to Get It) by Anthony J. Nownes (2006)

The Interest Group Connection: Electioneering, Lobbying, and Policymaking in Washington by P. S. Herrnson, R. G. Shaiko, et al. (2005)

http://www.opensecrets.org/lobbyists/index.asp

Documentary: http://www.pbs.org/moyers/moyersonamerica/capitol/lobby.html

First, the Dirt

If you watch the Moyers documentary (see box above) and look around the web for information on lobbying, you may come away with a not-very-nice opinion of lobbyists. Since 1998, 43 percent of the 198 Members of Congress who left government to join private life have registered to lobby. The *Washington Post* described these results as reflecting the "sea change that has occurred in lawmakers' attitudes toward lobbying in recent years." This sea change goes hand in hand with an increase in earmarking and the political use of earmarks, which are appropriations (funding for projects) that are written into funding bills without hearings or oversight. One recent spending bill included around 7,000 earmarks by one estimate, at a cost of several billion dollars. Earmarked items range from the relatively insignificant (but still maybe not the best use of federal funding) to the really big—from $100,000 for street furniture and sidewalks in a small town in Alabama to more than $200 million for the "bridge to nowhere" that would have replaced a ferry in Alaska (the project was scrapped after negative media attention).

While earmarking is legal, there have been a number of recent stories of the not-so-legal kind of lobbying activity. Just in the last few years newspapers gleefully reported former Representative Tom DeLay's indictments for shady campaign finance dealings, former Representative Randy "Duke" Cunningham's bribery conviction, and Representative William Jefferson's $90,000 in "frozen assets" (bribe money he accepted and kept in his freezer). The biggest of the recent scandals involved lobbyist Jack Abramoff and his fleecing of casino-rich Indian tribes and conspiring to bribe lawmakers. In 2006 Abramoff pled guilty to multiple felony counts related to the defrauding of American Indian tribes and corruption of public officials.

I asked Chris Andresen, who works for a lobbying group in Washington, about the public perception of lobbyists, and he agreed that the current perception of lobbyists in the media and in public opinion was very negative. His experience perhaps more accurately portrays the work of Washington lobbyists: "For the most part I think the work we do is very positive work. We have causes that we work on that we truly believe in and our clients believe in . . . I think it's just inaccurate to judge the whole lobbying world by the actions of a few actors like Abramoff. . . . Working in a firm like this I see what we're doing and how we're doing it and I think it's work that we can be proud of."

Where You'll Be

Students sometimes tell me what they really want to do is work for a lobbyist. What I often find is they actually want to work for an advocacy organization—two very different things. Like advocacy organizations, lobbying firms exist to persuade Congress and the agencies to act in a particular way. Unlike advocacy organizations, lobbying firms are first and foremost run for profit. As such, they are free to contribute to political campaigns, are typically much better funded (as they are paid very well by their clients), and work on a range of issues depending on the needs of their clients.

According to opensecrets.org, in 2007 companies spent $1.3 billion on lobbying, either hiring lobbying firms or hiring lobbyists to work in-house exclusively. Lobbyists, who must register and disclose who they work for and how much they got paid, work on just about every issue Congress considers. Their clients include cities and colleges, airports and corporations. Some of the work lobbyists do is not directly related to obtaining federal funding; a lobbyist might attend hearings and otherwise monitor an issue of interest to a client. Chris Andresen at Dutko Group offers this example:

> A nonprofit might just want to be more involved on the policy-making side—getting to know the Members and their staff so that they can have deeper relationships. For example, if you're a health care nonprofit we can connect you to people on the Hill you want to reach—congressional staff are inundated with stuff and if they have a health care issue and they have a relationship with a nonprofit that specializes in that particular issue, instead of having to do it on their own, they can call on that nonprofit for advice. Lots of nonprofits want to be involved and be helpful so with our help they can get to know the Member of Congress they want to work more with, maybe get media attention if that's what they're looking for, be recognized as a thought leader on a particular issue—it helps to raise their profile and lets them be part of the process.

In addition to creating relationships, lobbyists help their clients get funding either from a bill moving through Congress or from funding available from agencies. They may also try to change legislation or current law to help their clients. If, for example, their client is a big producer of some product overseas, they might try to change tax law to advantage their client. Or a university might want help improving the tax break students get when they start paying back their student loans.

If you have an interest in a particular topic, you would want to be sure the lobbyist you're considering works on that topic and represents clients whom you wouldn't mind helping. Also many lobbying firms have clear political leanings, based mostly on who their founding partners are (Republican or Democratic former Members of Congress).

What You'll Do

An intern at a lobbying firm is likely to analyze legislation, make deliveries to the Hill, attend and summarize hearings, and provide research assistance as necessary. Chris Andresen describes the typical work done by an intern at Dutko Group:

> It's a lot of research. For example there may be a new energy bill that a client is interested in, perhaps there are provisions that might not be good for them so the intern may be tasked to do an initial read of the bill, look at these specific provisions and then they're asked to present that research to people internally and in some cases directly to the client, depending on the level of trust that the people here have in the intern. . . . There are some office tasks—maybe 15 to 20 percent of their entire internship—and that's just part of the game too. I tell people coming in that they're going to have a really dynamic internship; you may come in one day and spend it entering contacts into someone's computer

but that will be unusual . . . interns are heavily involved in research and internal meetings, going to committee hearings and so on.

Another large lobbying firm described intern work as being comprised largely of making deliveries to the Hill, so you'll want to be clear what the typical assignments are before accepting an offer.

The People You'll Meet

Maybe more than any other group in Washington, lobbyists are about connections, connections, connections. They are useless to their clients if they can't pick up the phone and actually get through to committee staff, personal congressional staff, media contacts, and actual Members of Congress. If you prove yourself, you may be involved in meetings with those types of folks, who may prove useful to you as you move on in your career. You may also meet clients, which may open an unexpected door for you into some other sector such as business or local government.

What You'll Get

Chris Andresen at Dutko Group suggested that the perspective you gain at a lobbying firm is valuable in multiple ways: "In a lobbying firm, we're obviously very connected to Congress and our work patterns even follow Congress—when they're busy, we're busy, when they're out, we're slow. But this is also a business and so you get the political side of it but you also get to see the business side of it. So that gives interns an interesting view on things."

Congressional staff often parlay their experience into lucrative jobs in lobbying firms; making contacts and gaining an understanding of the work of these firms would likely ease this transition or eliminate it altogether for the enterprising intern. If you're set on a job on the Hill, lobbying experience is still valuable. As Chris at Dutko Group explains, "going from lobbying to the Hill gives you a different view. Once you're on the Hill and you get a call from a lobbyist, you sort of know what he's thinking or what his strategy is and I think that's really beneficial." Finally, unlike most Hill internships, these spots are more likely to be paid. More on paid and unpaid internships in the next chapter.

INTERNING IN A POLITICAL ORGANIZATION

GOOD BOOKS AND WEBSITES

Encyclopedia of American Political Parties and Elections by Larry J. Sabato and Howard R. Ernst (2007)
Presidential Elections: Strategies and Structures of American Politics by Nelson W. Polsby, Aaron Wildavsky, and David A. Hopkins (2007)
http://www.rnc.org
http://www.dnc.org

Where You'll Be

Up to this point, all the categories I've laid out are where you go if your interest is in the making of policy. If you are interested in how people get elected and you want to be a part of it, you have to work for a purely political organization, either in the public or the private sector. While you probably will get a sense of the political process working in Congress or for a lobbyist or a think tank/ advocacy group, the rules that govern campaigns and spending are very clear; Members of Congress and their staffs are not allowed to engage in political activity while they are being paid by taxpayer dollars and working in taxpayer-funded buildings. That work is done by the national committees, private firms, and some nonprofit political groups.

The political parties fund a number of different organizations to support political candidates. The national committees include:

- the central party committee (i.e., the Democratic National Committee and the Republican National Committee),
- the House campaign committee (i.e., the Democratic Congressional Campaign Committee and National Republican Congressional Committee),
- Senate campaign committee (i.e., the National Republican Senatorial Committee and Democratic Senatorial Campaign Committee).

In the private sector, political consultants are hired by campaigns to conduct polls, create media strategy, manage fundraising events, handle mail, and do a variety of other tasks. As for your physical work space, with so many kinds of political organizations, that will vary, but one student's advice is probably pretty accurate: "If you do anything campaign related, be prepared for very little in the way of space and comfort because they're spending their money on the campaign, not on the office."

What You'll Do

By all accounts, interning at the Democratic Congressional Campaign Committee (DCCC), the Republican National Committee (RNC), or similar organization is a fast-paced, in-the-thick-of-it experience. What an intern will actually do varies, depending on the department to which you are assigned, the timing of your internship vis á vis the election cycle, and the type of race you're working on. The DCCC's website has a good description of its departments and duties at http://www.dccc.org/get_involved/internships. Students should also consider working on an actual campaign, which might be anywhere in the country and is a great way to hit the ground running in politics.

Depending on the type of organization, interns may spend considerable time managing databases, conducting research, handling logistics, or manning phones. In fact, in the political world perhaps more than elsewhere in Washington, you must prove that you are committed to the cause (the party and/or the candidate) before you get any meaningful work. What that means in practice is that every intern will start with very menial, boring tasks. The ones that are enthusiastic about those tasks and are just thrilled to be there are the ones that move on to bigger and better things.

The People You'll Meet

The community of political operatives is a very small one, and there is a great deal of movement between organizations and firms, as campaigns start and end and opportunities open up. What this means for an intern is that your supervisor at your small political consulting firm could be the head spokesperson for one of the national committees by the time you come back for a job the following year. We'll talk more about that when we get to networking. Also, you're likely to at least be in the room with the candidate you're working for every once in a while, and you may get to meet other elected officials and party leadership in the course of your work.

What You'll Get

Of all the categories covered in this chapter, the work is the most intense and the hours are the longest working in politics. It can also be extremely exciting and rewarding; working even at the lowest level of a presidential campaign, regardless of what you do once your internship ends, will be something you remember for the rest of your life.

As in many internships, while the substance of what you will learn will prove invaluable should you choose to pursue a career path in this arena, it is the contacts that you make that will be the key. The world of political consulting is a small one, and, as we will discuss later, it is part of the ways of Washington to help people move along their career ladders.

CHAPTER 3

FINDING THE RIGHT INTERNSHIP

After reading Chapter 2, you should be able to narrow your search list to one or two categories. In addition to limiting your list by type of organization, you'll also want to think about topic areas that are of interest to you, what skills you have that will make you a stronger candidate, and you may wonder how your political views will affect your internship search. In addition to answering the above questions, the ultimate goal of this chapter is to help you identify internship opportunities and develop a list of potential internship sponsors. Campus-based, print, and online resources are discussed and a process is provided to help you identify your priorities for your internship experience. On the way, I also encourage you to think about ways to make yourself a stronger candidate, the implications of applying to (and working for) particular organizations, and thinking about which internships make the most sense for your career goals.

THINKING AHEAD: THE SKILLS YOU NEED

In the event that you are reading this earlier in your college years or even while you're still in high school, this next section may be very helpful to you as you develop a longer-range plan. If you are reading this in the spring of your junior year or later, these points may be helpful to you in thinking about what to highlight in your cover letter and resume.

Previous Experience

The experience section of your resume is important, but perhaps not in the way you might think. According to Liz Conroy in Senator Casey's office:

> For the interview, a lot of people come in and tell us all about the experience they have on political campaigns and so on. That sort of stuff is not as important as people might think it is. I like people who have shown dedication to a project or an idea, and that doesn't necessarily have to be a political project. I like to see a progression. For instance we're interviewing someone right now who decided he was very interested in economic development issues and so he approached a local commissioner who made him the lead on this youth campaign and he did marketing, polling, everything, and he showed us that he had an interest and he really went with it. And having a particular interest helps us assign students to the right team.

It is also the case that having one solid internship leads to another and another and ultimately to a job after college, and students are increasingly applying for internships much earlier in their college careers and in high school. Political consultant Michael Bassik shares this advice: "Any internship you can get going into college can be very helpful because then after your freshman year you're a much stronger candidate for better and better internships." A student concurs: "I think doing an internship on campus . . . is a great idea if you have that opportunity because it makes you a stronger candidate when you're going to Washington." Another student talks about the advantage, particularly in the political field, of starting your internship career early: "I think a freshman should know that it doesn't really matter how small you start off, it really helps to intern early. I spent my freshman year at the University of Florida and my first internship was this local congressional campaign for a candidate that had absolutely no chance in the world of winning but it was a foot in the door. After that I was able to get an internship with a gubernatorial campaign. So it really doesn't matter where you start, it's just a really good idea to get in the door early" (college senior).

I WISH I HAD KNOWN . . .

"I worked at a day camp for years every summer—my friends and I all did and every year we would say that next summer we would get a real job—a good internship—and even this last summer I wasn't at all organized and didn't apply to an internship until April so looking back I wish I had pushed myself a little harder early on to get some of these experiences." (college senior)

Finally, if you really want to do something off the wall for a summer but you don't want it to get in the way of future internships, consider this advice: "My advice to freshmen thinking about courses or internships is to do the things you like but it's really good to do something weird—things that make you stand out are a good thing. In my field, everyone studied Arabic and did security studies. So if you juggled for a summer that's kind of interesting and if you can talk about why you did something so different and what you got out of it that is a really good thing" (college graduate).

Language Skills

It's a good idea to have a background in a second language; that may be why so many universities require language courses. Having some ability in a second language opens up opportunities to work for organizations focused on particular regions or countries, even if you're not fluent. Having taken the courses suggests to potential sponsors that you are interested. Like the college graduate in the above quotation, the following student used an unusual language skill to stand out: "I took four semesters of Swahili and I just recently got accepted to a pretty tough internship and they said it was because they want me to work in the Africa department so that really helped" (college junior).

Another student found that just having a grounding in a romance language was useful in her work: "I think language classes are really important. A lot of the travel that the Secretary did was international and I found myself preparing biographies for the people he would be meeting with and using government websites that are in Italian and Portuguese and because I had taken a romance language, I was able to get what I needed. So that foundation was very important" (college senior).

Coursework

As mentioned in the first chapter, majoring in political science is not absolutely essential to doing well in Washington. In fact, numerous interview participants suggested that having a slightly different profile was helpful during the application process. According to Liz

Conroy in Senator Casey's office: "We strive to bring in a diversity of candidates. That includes what you're studying at school. We don't like to bring in 100% political science majors; we had two engineering and a biology major last term. Having a major other than political science makes them more competitive. We see millions of political science majors and we like to bring different perspectives to the table."

On the question of the importance of coursework, the responses in interviews varied. One student suggested that taking relevant coursework was more fun after coming back from Washington: "I didn't need a lot of classes before my Senate internship. It's almost more rewarding to take political science classes after your internship experience. I took one last semester and it was so much more meaningful because I had experiences that made the theory more real. You can do it either/or but I think doing the internship first was great" (college senior).

Another student felt that coursework wasn't particularly important to her employers: "I worked really hard to fit in a double major and as a result I didn't take any electives. After my internship experience this summer I realized no one really asked me what my major was and so maybe it helped but I regret that I didn't get a more varied educational experience" (college senior).

While some students didn't think coursework was particularly important, others did. For example, students interested in diplomacy or national defense might want to take particular courses in foreign policy or defense studies, just so they have a starting place, they have something to say during the interview, and their coursework reflects an interest in the topic. More specifically, students found that having a particular strength that set them apart was very helpful. "I think for me my biggest asset is that I'm studying engineering, which is very rare in Washington, and that has really helped me get some amazing internships" (college senior); "While I tried to take a variety of courses and have diverse experiences, I did find that specializing in East Asian studies really helped focus me and made me a good candidate for a very particular kind of internship that led to a full time job" (college graduate).

Several students commented on the quantitative aspects of their work in their internships, and wished they had been better prepared to interpret and work with harder data: "I think there's a quantitative side to all of the policy work that I think a lot of places think are important. And from a practical standpoint, I think even having just the introductory econ courses goes a long way to making you look more qualified and I think would help doing some of the work" (college senior).

Another student provides a perfect lead-in to our next topic, writing skills:

> I wish I had taken more political science courses that were more writing-based. Because I know applying for places there were a lot of applications that asked you to write about a political or policy issue that you think is relevant and current and what your stance is on it. And I had just taken a course on national security and so I wrote something very specific and I got the job and once I was there I asked what it was about my application that made me a good candidate and I was told the essay really did it. Because I was a rising sophomore and my coursework was just your average coursework and so the essay really set me apart. (college junior)

Coursework in any discipline that emphasizes writing skills may help you get a running start in Washington: "They loved that I have an English minor because writing is so important" (college junior).

Writing Skills

The ability to write well is possibly the most important skill you can have in Washington. People in Washington spend a great deal of time trying to communicate complex concepts and issues to a variety of audiences: Members of Congress, the media, voters. While many students have told me their writing improved immeasurably over the course of their internship, political consultant Michael Bassik explains the practical reason sponsors want students who can write well coming into the internship: "When it comes to writing, writing samples are required because writing is so important and if done poorly is really a timewaster; to have to rewrite something you might as well have done it yourself. Writing skills are very hard to pick up quickly so that is something that you should be thinking about from the outset of your college years: to learn how to be succinct and to the point and not beat around the bush is so critical especially in Washington."

Students interested in careers in journalism will benefit from knowing that the major newspapers require a substantial portfolio of published articles. One of these is the *Washington Post*. As you will see when you visit its website, former interns are now employed in the highest positions at the paper, and interns regularly have their stories published. Interns at the *Post* are paid—a very respectable $825 a week in summer 2007. Deadline is November 1. http://www.washpost.com/news_ed/summer_internships/index.shtml

WHEN TO START APPLYING

I WISH I HAD KNOWN . . .

"Lots of applications [deadlines] are very early, so knowing ahead of time about those internships—like planning to work on applications the summer before instead of waiting for January—I wish I had known about that." (college senior)

Some of the most interesting internships require considerable advanced planning. By the time you're done with the tasks laid out in this chapter you'll have a pretty good idea of when your internship search will begin just based on which organizations you're applying to. However, in addition to identifying your dream internships, you might also want to think a little strategically. I suggest the following approach:

1. At the end of the summer before you want to find an internship in Washington, spend some time developing your list of sponsors. In particular you are looking for those organizations with November deadlines (many of the media organizations and the more prestigious government agencies, such as the Department of State). Spend some time before heading back to campus getting those early applications together and even drafting cover letters for the positions with later application deadlines.

2. Apply to organizations with early deadlines the fall prior to your target summer.

3. In January or February you will start hearing back from the places you applied to in the fall (or you won't). If you weren't selected by any of those, revisit your list, check deadlines, and start applying to your second round of sponsors. Many sponsor deadlines are in March, so applying in January or February is appropriate.

4. As the actual deadlines approach for your second round of applications, call or email the internship coordinator to confirm receipt of your application (unless their website expressly says, "no calls").

5. Approximately two weeks after the application deadline passes you may call the internship coordinator to ask after the status of your application (again, only if that's not a problem for the sponsor—one student remembers calling a sponsor before she realized he was a "no calls" kind of sponsor and he was irate).

6. If you get no offers from either your first or second round, there are a number of smaller organizations (and even some of the bigger ones) with April deadlines. Make sure you have a few of those on your list as a fallback and apply as necessary.

SOURCES FOR INTERNSHIPS

There are a number of different places you can look for internship listings. Be forewarned; they are not typically organized in a cross-searchable way (for example, if you're looking for media jobs in Washington) and you'll have to track down up-to-date email addresses and contact names. Consider doing lots of this the August before and then coming back to do the finishing touches as deadlines approach; that way you won't have to spend hours and hours on internship cover letters at the same time as you are knee (or neck) deep in class work. Your first stop should be the career services office (or their website) at your college or university. I'll talk about what they offer, then I'll review the other sources of information on internships, including print resources, online resources, and actual people you know.

Your College Career Services Office

I have found that students do not always take advantage of the resources available through their college's career services office. Do not make this mistake. The career services office is there to help you be a success not only in your senior year as you start thinking about a full-time job but throughout your time in school. While the resources of a career services office will vary based on the size of the college and its budget, I encourage you to find out exactly what the office offers and take advantage of it all. For example, many offices have workshops on cover letter and resume writing, and some offices will make comments on your materials. They may also have a library that houses internship directories and they may have access to online internship directories, all of which are very useful to you. While most career services offices don't have the resources to match particular students with actual internships, some do. Even if they don't go that far, they may have a searchable database of alumni who have expressed a willingness to help students. If this is the case, you have a pool of potential sponsors who have a particular interest in supporting someone from their alma mater; I have been witness to this at Penn, where alumni have created positions expressly for a Penn student and have gone out of their way to ensure that the position is a meaningful one. Even if you don't find an internship with an alumnus, you may develop a mentoring relationship with someone who is in the field you are interested in and whom you can call upon when you have career questions. I created a formal mentoring program in Washington for Penn students and alumni, and many students have said that the mentoring experience was the most enriching part of their summer experience:

> For me, it was really useful to tap into the alumni from my college that were in the agencies. Actually it turned out that the Assistant Secretary chose me to intern for him because he was an alumnus from my college and I worked directly with him in his office and so that really gave me a leg up. As it went on, the people in the office went out of their way

to make sure I really got the full Washington experience so they set me up with a White House tour and made sure that I got to experience everything I could while I was there. (college senior)

I think it was really helpful to connect with alumni from my college who really were interested in helping me so connecting with alumni when you can is a great idea. (college junior)

NONCITIZENS AT U.S. COLLEGES

If you are a noncitizen, you are not eligible to work for the federal agencies, and many paid internships may also be off-limits. However, it is possible to find positions, particularly in the think tank and advocacy sectors. Policy on accepting noncitizens varies widely; you may want to come up with your ideal list of sponsors and then contact them to find out if they accept noncitizen applicants.

Regardless of where you apply, in order to work (including in an unpaid internship), you are required to secure an Employment Authorization Document. Most universities have a designated school official to help you through the process. Check with your college's career services office, which can point you in the right direction.

In addition to alumni and staff in your career services office, consider asking your professors if they have any suggestions for organizations to consider or contacts in Washington who may be able to help. Professors often communicate with practitioners, advocates, and staff on the Hill. If you have performed well in her class, this may be a good opportunity to visit her during office hours and pick her brain a bit. Also mention that you're looking for an internship to everyone you know; you never know who has a friend in Washington who would be happy to take you on.

I WISH I HAD KNOWN . . .

". . . that professors can be a really good window into internship opportunities. A lot of them have good perspectives and even contacts when it comes to particular internships and also can direct you to the right people. That's been very helpful to me in narrowing down what I want to do and where. But I never would have thought that my professors had connections to Washington and lots of them do and can be helpful." (college junior)

Print Resources

Unfortunately, there is no print resource specifically for Washington, D.C., internships. There are a few directories of internships; I'll talk about each in turn.

- *Vault Guide to Top Internships*: The most recent publication date is 2008, which makes it the freshest of the bunch. Sadly, it is organized alphabetically rather than by topic or region, which makes it an interesting Sunday browse but a little tedious if you have a more targeted search in mind. One of their indexes is by industry; their government category has about 100 listings and is a little random; international, national, and state internships are included but none of those categories are exhaustive. There is also oddly a public policy category with three listings. With 20,000 internships available in Washington every summer, this list won't get you terribly far, but it's a start.

- *The Internship Bible*: The most recent version is from 2005, so you'll need to double-check all the contact information, deadlines, and the like on sponsor websites. Like the *Vault Guide*, this directory is organized alphabetically, but its topic index is much more specific. So, for example, it has short lists for defense, nature, and so on. These may or may not be in Washington, which can lead to lots of fruitless page turning. The directory also has a geographic index with a couple hundred listings for Washington. There's probably some duplication with the *Vault* list, but worth looking through.

- *Yale Daily News Guide to Internships*: The most recent version appears to be for 2000, which is a bit dated, but this guide is arranged by field, which is helpful and so worth perusing. The chapter on politics and government includes many of the major organizations in Washington, but also includes lots of random organizations from across the country. There are about 120 listings in this chapter.

- *Peterson's Internships*: The most recent edition is 2004, and the book is organized by sector, which is good. Unfortunately, it does not include "public policy" as one of its topics, but there are several hundred entries in the geographic index under "District of Columbia," so it's well worth a look.

Online Resources

As you can easily find out for yourself via Google, there are plenty of sites that say they provide thousands of listings for free, but I have not found one that is as comprehensive as you need it to be. The free sites typically ask sponsors to submit openings or a statement about their ongoing internship program. Because no one is methodically building a database, the results are often spotty. I have checked all of these sites and, searching for internships limited to Washington, D.C., I've gotten results of a dozen internships or less from several of these sites. My favorite site is http://www. idealist.org. It seems to be well known particularly in the nonprofit/ advocacy sector. It has a database of organizations which includes links to their websites. It also lists actual job/internship openings submitted by the organizations. In addition to being a good place to start your search, it's a handy site if you get to March and are feeling like you might want to apply to a few more places but you don't want to apply to places if their spots are already filled.

Here's a list of a few other online resources to get you started:

- http://www.idealist.org: Again, a great place to look, particularly if you're interested in advocacy work. My search here came up with 302 listings.
- http://www.internshipprograms.com: I searched for all internships in Washington, D.C., and it came up with about fifty, mostly in the nonprofit/advocacy sector.
- http://www.monstertrak.com: I restricted my search to government and policy and Washington, D.C., and it came up with three listings. Not sure that's worth your search time.

There are also two subscription databases that you might want to use. Your college or university may be subscribers; check with them for access information.

- http://internships.com: I searched for all internships in Washington, D.C., and it came up with 1,500 results. Unfortunately, the list doesn't appear to be organized in any way, even alphabetically, and there is no way to drill down into that search. One nice feature of this search engine is it allows you to search by compensation (paid/unpaid).

- http://internships-usa.com: This database has a list just for Washington, though again you can't specify exactly what you're looking for, which means you have to plow through the whole list, and many of the entries are for law students only.

Full-Service Options

Finally, there is a way to take the legwork out of finding a D.C. internship, but (of course) it's not cheap. The Washington Center (http://www.twc.edu) is a full-service program that finds the internship for you, arranges for credit with your home university, allows you to take courses while in Washington, and sets up your housing. The program cost, including about $3,000 for housing, is about $9,000.

GETTING PAID

As you consider whether to go through the process on your own or hire someone to do it for you, you might also be wondering about how likely it is that you'll find a paid position. Across the board, about half of internships in the United States are paid. This varies widely, however, by industry and city, and even within industries. For example, while it has been suggested that "glamour industries" (television, politics) are less likely to offer paid internships because the demand for those internships is so great, there are lots of high-demand internships in Washington that pay pretty well and lots of them that don't. For example, the *Washington Post* offers a very generous stipend for their internship, which involves researching and writing stories that actually get published. *USA Today*, however, offers a stipend of only $200 a month for a very similar experience, and other media outlets offer no pay at all. The same is true in politics and other fields. The bottom line is, the value of an internship to you in the long term is not at all related to how much you get paid, and you're much better off looking for an internship that will contribute to your understanding of an industry and help you make contacts, and if you get paid, consider it a bonus.

WHERE TO APPLY—AND HOW MANY APPLICATIONS TO SEND

Having read this far in the chapter, you know where to look for internships and you have a timeline for starting the search process. As you develop your list, as mentioned before, you may want to spread your applications so that you have a few early deadlines, a few middle deadlines (February/March), and a few late deadlines. You also want to be sure you apply to enough organizations. Somewhere between ten and fifteen applications seems to be the right number for most students. This varies based on what you're looking for and how much competition there will be. For example, if you are politically conservative, at least in my experience you may have a little less competition. The students I have worked with who have applied to conservative organizations tend to apply to fewer organizations and get more offers, possibly because there are fewer young conservatives than young liberals. Also, if you're focusing on a very popular issue (foreign policy, for example) or setting your sights on only the most prestigious organizations, you'll have to apply to more organizations. You may want to consider the competitiveness of the programs you are applying to and make sure you've got a few on your list that are a little easier to get into, and preferably these will have later deadlines. Some of the print resources usefully tell you how many applicants the programs typically get and how many are accepted. If you are at all interested in working in the House or the

Senate, you should definitely apply. Unless you come from a district that gets lots and lots of applicants (those that are closer to Washington or those with very popular elected officials), as a constituent you have a good chance of being accepted. House deadlines are typically in March, though many are rolling, which means they'll take constituent applicants as early as January or February. Senate deadlines vary, and most are more competitive just due to the numbers of constituents. On the Senate side they often split their summer program into two six-week sessions, which allows them to offer more positions to more constituents. Whatever you end up doing, do not apply to organizations as a backup if you aren't willing to accept their offer before hearing back from other places you applied; understandably, you'll only have a day or two at most to consider an offer. Don't waste an internship coordinator's time and get in the way of other applicants if you're really not willing to work for that three-person shop whose focus is an issue that only marginally interests you. Some people might be willing to accept such a position because really they just want to be in Washington or they really want to work on that issue or they like the idea of a small organization; if you're not one of them, don't apply. The other factor you should be certain about going in is if you're willing to take an unpaid position. If you really, really can't, then don't apply to them.

In addition to pay, competitiveness, and deadlines, you need to think about your political inclinations and how they fit with your potential sponsor's politics.

Crossing the Aisle

Unlike other cities, one major factor in deciding where to apply for an internship in Washington is your political party affiliation. If you have a clear sense of that, you're frankly much better off, for a couple of reasons. On a practical level, being clear on your politics helps you narrow your options considerably. For example, you've decided you want to work for a think tank and you vote a straight Democratic ticket. This means you can strike Heritage Foundation, American Enterprise Institute, and lots of others off your list and focus your application efforts on places like the Brookings Institution, the Progressive Policy Institute, Third Way, Center for American Progress, and so on. The other reason you're better off if you have a good sense of what your politics are is that you don't want to get an internship with a progressive organization only to discover that you love Washington and want to make a career of it, but you are more comfortable with the conservative agenda. While you may gain some useful office experience and an understanding of how a think tank functions, going forward, the contacts you will have made won't be terribly useful to you, and you'll have to explain to prospective employers why you're crossing the aisle (spend some time watching C-Span if you don't know what I mean by "crossing the aisle"; you'll see that the Republicans are on one side of the main aisle and the Democrats are on the other). When I was a legislative director to a Democratic Member of Congress, competition for each advertised position was pretty fierce. I suspect things haven't changed much, and if anything the competition is greater given the larger numbers of college students today. Here's how I sorted through the pile of resumes; first, I got rid of everyone without any work experience. If you've done an internship or two or if you've had an office job, you would still be in the "possible" pile. Second, I got rid of everyone whose experience was with a Republican Member of Congress or a conservative organization. After that I would look for candidates from my Member's home state (and preferably city) and candidates with experience in the particular issues the position would be responsible for. The bottom line is, with lots of competition, coming from the other party is a great way to get sorted out of the pile, which means you'll never get a chance to explain your change of heart. Erin Green at the Center for American Progress also acknowledges that politics can be a problem: "I've known people who have worked for one party and then changed their mind and wanted to work for the other party and they can't do it. It's very difficult to explain that in Washington." Michael Bassik concurs: "I would be very hesitant to hire a Republican, even if they just interned for a Republican. I would have to explain to a variety of people why we should hire this person. If you think you want a career in Washington, don't work for someone from the other party."

Chris Andresen at Dutko Group offers some even more nuanced advice when thinking about what kind of internship on the Hill you want to consider if you think you might like to eventually find a job with a lobbyist: "If you've worked on the Hill for someone on the far left or far right, that might taint you if you're trying to get into a lobbying world. These days in Washington you really need to be able to work both sides of the aisle in order to get anything done. You need to be able to work for Republicans and Democrats. So if you have relationships on both sides, that's a really valuable asset."

If you really don't know where your politics will come down yet, try working for a less politicized organization, like a lobbyist (who works for both), or in a nonpolitical job in an agency. You should know that trying to avoid politics is tough; most advocacy organizations and think tanks, while they all say they are nonpartisan on their website, are really on one side or the other of the political divide. The same is true for many media outlets.

A POLITICS PROBLEM

What if you've decided your dream internship is in the House of Representatives, but you are a Republican and your Member of Congress is a Democrat? If you're planning on a long and exciting career in Congress, that could be tricky. Here are a few ideas. First, check the Senate; if one of your Senators is Republican, you should definitely apply to her. Staff movement back and forth between the Senate and the House isn't terribly common (everyone thinks their side is the place to be) but as long as you're in the right party, your Senate internship should come in handy should you decide to pursue an entry-level job in the House later on. The other option is to contact the Members of Congress who are Republican from the districts surrounding yours; some congressional offices get more applications to their internship program from constituents than they can handle, but some may have a spot or two open and are happy to have an intern who at least knows the region, if not the specific constituency. Feel free to say that your politics don't match the Member who represents your district; Republicans and Democrats both like to look after their own on the Hill. The other possibility is trying for an internship in your party's leadership office—the Speaker or the minority leader, depending on what your party is and which party currently has the majority in the House.

FINDING THE FIFTEEN

This exercise may help you as you develop your list of fifteen sponsors to which you will be applying. Circle the appropriate choices and try to stick to them as you start coming up with your list. The more categories you start with, the harder it's going to be to choose from the large number of internships your search will yield. Politics and salary also may help you narrow your list.

Category
   House
   Senate
   White House
   Agencies
   Nonprofits
Preferred Issue:
   Think tanks
Preferred Issue:
   Political
   Media

Political affiliation
   Republican/Conservative
   Democrat/Liberal
   Libertarian

Salary
   Paid
   Unpaid

CHAPTER 4

LANDING THE INTERNSHIP

This chapter guides you through the nuts and bolts of applying, following up, interviewing, and accepting an offer. While much of the guidance provided in this chapter could pertain to any job application process, the advice is tailored to the particular nature of the Washington internship universe, where a final offer can often be contingent on obtaining top secret security clearance, one internship position announcement can get hundreds of applicants, and hiring decisions are typically made after a telephone rather than an in-person interview. The chapter includes discussions with a range of internship sponsors on how they choose from the many applications they receive, focusing on the skills and experiences they look for in their first round of candidates.

BEFORE YOU WRITE

Before we get to actually writing cover letters, there are a few things that you'll want to do before you send out your first letter. First, you'll want to make sure your online presence is not going to detract from the image you're trying to present to employers. Employers today certainly might take a minute to pop your name in a Google search and see what comes up. They might even look at Friendster, MySpace, or Facebook. While no employer should expect to hire angels (you are college students, after all), they also don't want to see evidence of behavior that really is in poor taste. Michael Bassik offers this advice: "There's a great deal of discussion in D.C. these days about being careful about what you put on your MySpace/Facebook entry. I know people who check them before making a hiring decision. I would just monitor the privacy settings and just be careful what's public. It's a new age and we're in a transition period and employers really don't know what to make of these public pages but I would say just be cautious, be cautious about what pictures are up there."

Others suggest an even more conservative approach, limiting the type of content that's publicly available to the squeaky-clean kind (hobbies, interests), not posting pictures of you anywhere near drugs or alcohol, and making sure your friends don't provide links to evidence of debauchery. How far you take it is really up to you, and may depend on the type of internship you're considering. For example, a small advocacy organization whose average staff age is twenty-three may not mind what you have posted, while the State Department might.

The other thing you'll want to do before starting the application process is to line up your references. Application requirements range from an emailed cover letter and resume (which is very common) to an online application with all kinds of attachments, like writing samples and references or letters of recommendation. Certainly before you list anyone as a reference it's always a good idea to tell them you're doing so. Michael Bassik offers advice on that part of the process: "Just be very aware of who you are asking to act as a phone reference. I've been asked to act as a phone reference by individuals who really surprised me because I wasn't someone who was going to give them a great reference. Definitely ask if they would be willing to act as a reference and would they be willing to say positive, wonderful things about you."

If the places you're applying to require a letter of recommendation, do as much as you can for the person you are asking to write the letter. For example, after he agrees to send a letter on your behalf, you might email him a first draft of the letter. Even if you are not comfortable writing the substance of the letter yourself (and your writer is likely to have a letter that he recycles), it wouldn't hurt to provide a preformatted template, with the name of the person the letter is going to, the address, and so on. You'll also want to tell him in your email if there are particular points or qualities that you are hoping to highlight in your application, so that if he can speak to those things, he will. If the letter has to be mailed, send your letter writer an addressed and stamped envelope as soon as he agrees to write the letter for you.

THE PERFECT RESUME

If your college career services office offers resume help, you must take full advantage of that opportunity. You should also be open to constructive criticism. I am sometimes surprised by students who, after I suggest they have another go at their resume, tell me that it has gotten them this far and they think it's fine. These students might have the same experience as one student interviewed for this book: "My supervisor looked at my resume and she just ripped it apart. I thought it wasn't so bad but I had no idea." While career services will help, here are some basics. On length, current college students should be able to fit everything on one page. I've been in lots of jobs and have publications and presentations and can still fit everything on two pages. Be concise, and also think about structuring the resume so the most relevant information is the first thing they will read. For example, you probably don't need to list all the honors you got when you were in high school first; you can leave those to the end if you have room and if you think they say something about what kind of person you are. State your educational experience, then get right to your work experience.

Internship sponsors are not as a rule looking for significant work experience on a college student's resume. They may, however, be looking for some evidence of commitment to a cause. For example, Erin Green at the Center for American Progress says, "Work experience is not a must but if for example they're volunteering or doing something that shows an interest in the thing they're applying for, that's good. We want to know they're not just applying to us randomly." Political consultant Michael Bassik offers advice along similar lines: "If your resume includes some political experience, then your resume is going to go right to the top. And it's not that I'm looking for particular skills or experiences, but it gets to the interest/passion level you show. Even if they've volunteered once for a political campaign it shows passion. I'm not expecting that they wrote press releases and came up with strategy; they might have been answering phones, but having that little bit of political passion is key."

With work experience/volunteering taking up the bulk of the page, the end of the document should list relevant extracurricular activities, language ability, and travel experience (again, only if relevant). Your font should be something fairly traditional, like Times New Roman, and your headings should be the same font and bold, with a font size of twelve.

THE COVER LETTER

I try to do three things in my cover letters. One is introduce myself, two is why they need me and three is why I need them. Because if you can convince them that it's going to be a mutually beneficial relationship and they can see where they're going to help you further your career and you're going to help them, and you can do that in a well-written, concise way, they're going to respond to that. (college senior)

While the task of writing cover letters is despised by job applicants the world over, they really are a great way to convey who you are, why you are valuable to your potential internship sponsor, and what you want to get from the experience. While the first two things might also be evident in your resume, your particular interest in that organization will not. Your cover letter is your chance to tell them. According to Erin Green at the Center for American Progress, "Cover letters are important to express what you think we are and why you want to work for us. People who are enthusiastic about the work we do tend to get looked at." This idea is echoed by Liz Conroy in Senator Casey's office: "A lot of times when writing Capitol Hill cover letters a lot of people ignore who they are actually writing their cover letter to; whose office they're applying to work in. We get a lot of generic 'I just want to work on the Hill' kind of letters. I like to see that you've looked at our website, you know what the Senator stands for—that doesn't mean that you necessarily line up position-wise with the Senator but something about this office that makes me think there's a reason you're applying to our office versus other offices."

It's also important to recognize that internship sponsors are not just looking for cheap or free labor; they want to make an investment in and support young people who are considering careers in public service. If you can express what it is about the experience that will help you as you think about your career path, that will tell them that their efforts to provide a substantive experience will not be wasted on you.

In terms of style and content, you certainly want to stand out from the crowd, and several students talk about how they accomplish that. One student, however, suggests that it's a fine line, and points out the risk when you are trying to stand out in your cover letter: "One of my tasks this summer was to sort resumes for the next intern group and so I got a different perspective on the hiring process and I think just the really basic nuts and bolts of writing is so important. Not trying to be over the top. A lot of the time that sort of writing would get them weeded out right away—being too outlandish, or in sort of a gimmicky way. I think that sometimes people feel like they really need to stand out in their cover letter and I think sometimes that backfires on them." Your cover letter should be personal, well researched, and well written. It should reflect who you really are, not who you think the employer wants you to be. Aim for thoughtful rather than splashy.

If you feel there is something brief you can attach that speaks to your writing ability, you should consider doing so. One student found success using this strategy: "I think I was helped by including supplemental writing samples. So my cover letter was pretty low-key but then I attached a couple of things that had been published so they could really see how I write" (college senior).

On format, as for your resume, keep it simple, stick to one page, and be conservative with your font choice. Don't try to decrease your font to get more words in; if it can't be easily read, that's a good enough excuse to toss it out. In three paragraphs you should be able to summarize who you are and what you're looking for from the internship and what it is about the organization that you like. As much as you can, you want to personalize the letter so that it's different from the hundreds of letters they will get. One college senior suggests the following: "I've used anecdotes and stories of how certain events have shaped my life and how this position really fits in with that and that seems to work." In your concluding paragraph, you may also want to mention your available start and end dates and how best to contact you. Of course, for an internship where writing is important, this letter should be very carefully written, the grammar should be perfect, and there should be no typos. One last bit of advice on content: "I think it's important not to spend too much time in your cover letter talking about what's on your resume since they can just look at the resume for that" (college junior). Your cover letter is important and shouldn't look like a rush job. Consider writing cover letters the summer before you intend to go to Washington, even if deadlines are in the spring.

APPLYING TO CONGRESSIONAL OFFICES

When applying to your Member of Congress, use the following address line:

To a Senator:
> The Honorable (full name)
> United States Senate
> Washington, DC 20510
> Attn: (first, last name), Internship Coordinator

> Dear Mr./Ms. (Last Name):

To a Representative:

    The Honorable (full name)
    United States House of Representatives
    Washington, DC 20515
    Attn: (first, last name), Internship Coordinator

    Dear Mr./Ms. (Last Name):

    Call the office to get the name of the internship coordinator. Even if it's on the website, it doesn't hurt to call and confirm; staff changes at that level are frequent. Make sure to read up on the Representative/Senator on his website so that you can make an informed comment in your cover letter. Also be sure to follow website instructions exactly, giving them no chance to toss your application out at the first round.

One Letter, Fifteen Applications?

With the prospect of writing fifteen cover letters ahead of you, it might be tempting to write one cover letter that suits them all and then just change the addressee information. As previously mentioned, that's not a terribly good idea, as readers like to think that you aren't just randomly applying to them. The students I interviewed all agreed that a generic letter was a recipe for failure:

> I just was in a friend's dorm room recently and she was preparing cover letters for DC and she had this very generic letter where she was just basically changing the name of the organization she was applying to and I feel like that's what a lot of people who apply to these jobs are doing. So if you just personalize your letters a little bit that may really set you apart. (college junior)

If you're applying to a bunch of organizations in a similar field it's really tempting to just change the name of the organization but you really should personalize the letter—something about the company or that position that you find really interesting—at least they know you spent some time looking and thinking about it. (college junior)

Even if you are recycling parts of your letter from other applications, make sure the recycled letter fits the new application perfectly. One student skipped this step and lost her shot at a very good internship I had recommended her for because her letter was all about how she perfectly met the requirements of some other internship.

SECURITY CLEARANCE

As mentioned in the section in Chapter 2 that talks about working for a federal agency, some of the internships in federal agencies require security clearance. A typical clearance process takes six to nine months, which is why their deadlines are earlier in the year (often in November). While the level of security clearance and the intensity of the process varies by agency, if security clearance is required you'll need to provide details about every address you've ever had, every employer, every school attended, and names of neighbors and teachers. They will check your criminal record, ask for fingerprints, and will probably require a drug test. The process is also a little mysterious, perhaps appropriately. Every year students tell me about clearance processes that happened and they never even heard the results or were never contacted by anyone to be told that they were cleared. Several students interviewed for this book had that experience:

Security clearance is unnerving because they don't really

tell you when you pass your clearance. You have to figure out lots of things to prepare for being in Washington and security clearance can really hold you up. (college senior)

I don't know how I got security clearance because I was never contacted by anyone, no one I put down on my list was ever contacted, I never got drug tested—I don't know what they looked at but I got an email in mid-May telling me that I had passed. (college junior)

The other possibly tricky part about clearance is that every agency has its own standard for clearance. For example, one agency might require that you haven't taken any illegal drugs in the past three years, while another agency might have a problem with your ever having taken illegal drugs at all.

While all of that does sound daunting, it's much easier for students to get clearance than permanent candidates, for several reasons. First, compared to a thirty-year-old job applicant, a college student will probably have a more straightforward profile: fewer addresses and employers, fewer things that need explaining. Second, interns often get provisional or temporary clearance, which is easier to process. Also on the positive side, if you are interested in this line of work, once you have clearance it is much easier to get clearance in the future, which makes you a more attractive job candidate.

SCARY SECURITY STORIES

"On the second day at the Pentagon I was asked to do the mail run and I went into this room and there are fancy LCD screens on the wall and guys with guns and so I go to this guy and ask for the mail. This guy's mouth drops open, then he asks what office I'm from and then calls my office and asks why I'm in a secure room which is actually where they receive top secret classified cables from submarines. So now I have a red flag on my security record." (college junior)

"I was working in the Pentagon and I had a card to swipe in and so I'm swiping in one day and was having trouble and a gentleman walked up and asked if I needed help and I said no and I eventually got it and he followed me in once I got through and that's actually a big deal because you're not supposed to let anyone come in behind you, everyone has to swipe in. Well I didn't know that, so I came in and this guy came in and he walked around a bit and then left. And then he immediately knocked on the door and asked to speak to the security manager, and it turned out this guy was testing security and basically I was busted. So now I have a flag on my security clearance." (college graduate)

"I was working in an annex of the State Department and on my second day I used my swipe card to go in and sirens start going off. I knew the PIN was somewhere in the secretaries' desk but I didn't want to be rooting around the desk when the security staff arrived so I just stood in the middle of the room and waited—it was a little scary!" (college junior)

If you are planning on pursuing a position that requires clearance, just know that if there is anything complicated about your background, it may hold your clearance up, which may mean you won't be able to start the internship when planned, or even at all. One student relates a friend's experience with clearance: "I'm going through security clearance now and it's really intense. You have to give them fingerprints, and they ask you all kinds of questions. I have a friend whose father is Persian and he didn't get cleared in time for last summer, but he finally got cleared and they're giving him an internship this summer so especially if there's anything a little different about your background it can really slow things down" (college junior).

One helpful thing to know about the clearance process is that agencies typically honor their internship offers even if the clearance process delays your ability to participate. I have had students start their internships well into June, while others were told that they wouldn't get cleared in time for the coming summer but they were promised a slot for the following summer.

WRITING SAMPLE

On the application side, I think the writing sample was a big deal. I think having a good writing sample—having something to show them that's a really strong writing sample is important. (college junior)

We have talked a bit in earlier chapters about the importance of good, clear writing; the writing sample is your opportunity to show you're coming in with strong writing skills. Some sponsors may ask you to write something on a particular topic, though that's less common. More typically, if they ask for a writing sample at all they will ask you to submit somewhere between three and five pages of a paper that you've done for a class. As most of your papers are likely to be in the ten- to twenty-page range, you'll have to take an excerpt. Remember that the goal of Washington writing is to relate complex material succinctly and clearly. While some of your papers may do that all the way through, some may ramble on a bit; I suggest you not send those parts. Look at your introduction and conclusions; that may show a progression of analysis and they should be summaries of all the pages in between. Don't worry too much if they're not policy-oriented, though obviously the more related they are to a policy issue, the better.

ON WAITING FOR A CALL

You've submitted your applications and now you're wondering what will happen next. The following student account explains why the timeline offered earlier suggests you call to make sure your application was received:

> This past summer I applied in February to a bunch of places and come April I figured it was time to make a phone call because I never even heard if they received my resume. So I called one of them and they said oh, perfect, when do you want to start and it was like they had meant to email me but hadn't gotten around to it. A similar thing happened to me the summer before—the coordinators don't feel the same time pressure that we feel when it comes to April and we still haven't heard from internship sponsors about applications because we still have to find housing and make plans. So definitely follow up and make sure your application got there and don't feel bad about sending a polite email saying you just wanted to be sure they got your materials and thanking them for their time. I don't think anyone's going to be upset about that and it's just very important because otherwise you're sitting there, wondering what's going on and that's not a good feeling.

Several of the students interviewed for this book got to know their internship coordinators in a way that you won't be able to until you get to Washington. What they found were lots of people who were a lot like them:

> Just a follow up email is so important. I worked with a think tank and we meet a lot of the other think tank interns and coordinators and for most of the coordinators, that's not their main job. It's a side job that they have to do in addition to their main job. And they're also very young; the ones I met were all younger than 25. And they had a lot of other stuff to do. But because most of them were only two or three years out of college, they could really sympathize. So don't be intimidated because the fact is, most of the coordinators are not really organized on the internship front just because they have so much else to do, but they don't mind responding to an email. (college senior)

As the timeline in the last chapter suggested, there are two opportunities for you to place a call. First, a few days before the deadline you may want to call (or email) the internship coordinator to make sure they received your materials. Thank them very much, tell them you're really excited about this internship and you hope to hear from them soon. Once the deadline that they have posted on their website has passed (that is, a week or, preferably, two later), depending on how the first call or email went, you might want to give the internship coordinator a call or email and ask very politely if she has finalized her summer hiring decisions. Stay positive, be brief, and don't ask for a yes or no answer; give them a chance to consider you.

THOUGHTS ON THE INTERVIEW

Between two and four weeks after you submit your application to an organization's internship program, you may be called for a telephone interview. This is very good news; as most D.C. internships don't require an in-person interview, a phone interview means you've made it to the final round! Here are a few suggestions that might help get you through the call and to an offer.

First, let's talk about the challenges of a phone interview. Just because you're not putting your only suit on and going to someone's office doesn't mean you can relax. You need to sound like you mean business and you need to have thought a bit about what you are going to say. Erin Green at the Center for American Progress offers this advice: "In a phone interview I want a student to be well prepared. They should know about us. They should be on a phone that's going to work and not cut out, and they should be in a quiet place. If they know about some report that we've put out, that's a good sign."

In addition to making sure you can hear and be heard and not be interrupted (don't give them a cell number to call you on—give them a land line number), you want to make sure you communicate a positive attitude. Usually this is communicated through body language in a face-to-face interview; sitting up straight, making eye contact, and smiling communicate to the person you're speaking to that you are fully engaged in the conversation and you're a bright and energetic person. When you're interviewing by phone, try to relay as much of this as you can in your voice. It will help to sit up straight at a desk with a pen and paper (not in front of a keyboard— you don't want them to hear you tapping away and think you're checking your email) and smile when you speak—a positive tone can be very convincing. Part of that positive attitude is expressing enthusiasm about the position or the organization or the cause—whichever you feel most. Chris Andresen offers these thoughts on the interview:

> I put a lot of stock in the interview. If I can get a face-to-face I absolutely take it. I look for someone who is well spoken and is comfortable getting into specifics. I like the students that have an interest outside of school that gives them a passion—that sets them apart. Someone who is active outside of school shows motivation, good time management skills—student government is a really good thing, volunteering, getting out on a campaign, something that shows that they have a special interest in politics. Because once you get here, you can't escape politics. So if people really love politics they'll like it here. I just feel like if they're smart and motivated they can pick up the research skills they need.

Liz Conroy in Senator Casey's office looks for enthusiasm but also a willingness to take advantage of the opportunity: "Students who have shown that they can complete a project, that they can bring in knowledge and experience, they can be clear about what they would like to accomplish while they are with us are strong candidates. We have an abundance of resources here in the Senate but you can also sit here and do data entry and sort mail and never do anything else if you're not going to take the initiative and do it yourself. So those are the qualities I'm looking for. You're able to use resources around you and will make real use of this experience."

Similarly but perhaps more forcefully, political consultant Michael Bassik offers this advice:

I always say that there's no prerequisite to work in politics. It's not like if you want to be an economist you need an economics degree; in order to intern in politics you just need to have an interest in politics. Because of that it's incredibly competitive, because anyone from any discipline can compete. In an interview, passion would be the key. There's not a specific set of skills. Assuming a candidate has basic office skills what we then look for is passion. Passion about politics, passion, passion, passion, it's the most important thing. Someone who is energized and excited and you can see it on their face speaks volumes about this individual.

Another aspect of having a positive attitude is expressing a willingness to do all kinds of assignments, including the boring ones. Says Erin Green from the Center for American Progress: "The intern on the phone interview that tells me they will only do some limited amount of menial tasks—even though our interns spend about 80 percent of their time on substantive projects, saying that on the phone interview is just not going to work. I feel very strongly that they're not just interns here to do the boring jobs. But it's important to have a good attitude. Those are the people that I remember—the ones that are helpful and want to learn everything—they're the ones that succeed."

Along the same lines, you want to let your supervisor know that you know you're just starting out and have plenty to learn. For high-achieving students it can be a challenge, but you want to be a little bit humble. Several internship sponsors I've talked to have told me that they don't respond well to students who don't recognize where they are in the pecking order. For example, if a prospective intern comes to the interview and says that she plans to run for Congress one day (soon) and she is a very good speechwriter, as an internship sponsor you tend to worry that you're going to have to rein this person in for eight or ten weeks, and that she won't be willing to take whatever assignment is available and needs to be done. Liz Conroy in Senator Casey's office is one of several sponsors who expressed frustration with this kind of candidate: "I get very turned off by those folks—we have a lot of candidates who have lots of political experience and they like to come in here and act like they know everything about it—you know, this is what I can bring to this office. I would rather hear, this is my experience, this is what I think I can do but this is what I want to learn. So I've seen a lot of kind of grandstanding and that doesn't work well."

As in any interview, you want to think about your answers to some broad questions about yourself, your experience, and your goals and expectations. You don't want to repeat what's on your resume; you need to add something to it that shows the experiences on your resume are helping you define your career goals. Think about answers to the following questions:

- Why do you want this internship?
- What will you bring to this internship that others won't?
- What past experience do you think will help you in this internship?
- What do you hope to learn by the end of this internship?

As discussed in the section on writing the cover letter, you should learn what you can about the organization to which you are applying. According to Erin Green at the Center for American Progress, "Our interns do a lot of real work for us. So we want people who actually know about us. One thing that is a no-no in an interview is to have someone ask questions that are answered on our website." Many students I spoke to found this to be true in other types of organizations as well. According to a college junior, "If you're applying to a federal agency and probably other places, they expect you to know a little about where you're applying. During my phone interview they asked me what I knew about their work and I was able to talk enough about that to get the job."

I WISH I HAD KNOWN . . .

While direct questions on your political background are unusual, it's not a bad idea to prepare a response. "I was surprised by some of the questions I got in the interview. I thought I was applying for a job and I didn't realize I was also applying for a [political] party. So for example I was asked for what policies or issues my position was different from the party and what my position was on abortion. All these things that I thought were tangential to my ability to sort mail. I was a little taken aback at first. I guess I wish I had known going in that they were going to ask about my political background." (college junior)

Also be prepared for the very common question "Do you have any questions for me?" If this hasn't been answered already, something along the lines of "While I recognize that much of the work I'll be doing will be administrative in nature, can you give me an example of a substantive project I might be assigned?" will open the door to talking about "real" work without seeming pushy. This is an important question, according to one student interviewed: "Ask specifically what tasks you would do with this job. I think applicants are often afraid to ask that question, but I know people who have been very disappointed when they actually got to the job because they didn't expect to be doing the tasks they were assigned. And particularly in Washington where the place you're working can be very glamorous and the internship can be not very glamorous.

So I think it's important to know what you're getting into" (college senior).

Now is also the time to find out how the program is structured; are you assigned to a particular staffperson or is there a "pool" of interns that get doled out work? Ask as well if attending speaking events or a congressional hearing that is of particular interest to you will pose a problem for them—that will get you to a conversation about working hours and also other speaking opportunities and events that they might make available to you. Just make sure you're clear that you're not talking about making field trips part of your daily experience and that you will absolutely work however many hours they expect you to, but you want to make sure you take advantage of being in Washington to be exposed to speakers that are relevant to your career path.

Whatever your questions are and however you answer their questions, be prepared to do most of the talking. While in some cases you find the sponsor is doing most of the talking just because that's who they are, most sponsors feel the interview is an important opportunity to get to know you. According to Liz Conroy in Senator Casey's office: "On the phone interview, I really want to hear about the student and their interests. I sometimes really have to push and ask questions and I get a one-word response. I really need to get a feel for who this person is and the only way to do that is for the candidate to talk more than I do."

In addition to making sure you say enough, you'll need to prepare to be on the phone with a Washingtonian. Washington is a busy place for just about everyone who works there; it's a place where lots of powerful people are making lots of important decisions. Sometimes that leads to people who seem to be constantly rushed and obviously thinking about all the other things they need to be doing. On a phone interview (and certainly in person), that might rattle you. Remember that even though they might not sound it, they really do want to know a bit about you: "My interview went well—the challenge was my interviewer was very obviously in a hurry; I think she was trying to interview all the candidates in like an hour and so she was really rushing. I tried not to get rushed by that and explain what I wanted to do and why I wanted to do it and I think it's important for them to know that they're not wasting their time on you and even though they're in a hurry you need to not get rushed and as a result not represent yourself very well" (college senior).

As soon as your interview ends, send a thank-you note. You can always send an email (and that may be best where mail is delayed due to security screening, as in the House or Senate), but increasingly a mailed letter is considered going the extra mile. Either way, do it immediately after you finish your interview. As soon as you hear that your phone interview has been scheduled, get a stamp and appropriate stationery and be ready to send that thank-you note the same day. You might want to process the interview a bit; think about how well you feel you expressed yourself and if there was anything you would have liked to say but didn't. The following text is a sample that you can adapt to your own needs.

Sample Thank-You Letter

I appreciate your taking the time to speak to me about the internship position available at [organization name]. I am excited about the opportunity to intern with such a well-regarded organization.

The internship, as you presented it, seems to be an excellent match for my skills and interests. I am confident that my coursework in [subject] and my experience as [position title] will enable me to be a productive member of your staff. I was interested to learn in our conversation that [interesting tidbit], and would very much like to be involved in [opportunity]. In addition to my enthusiasm, I will bring to the position a willingness to learn about both your organization and the public policy field.

I am very interested in the internship at [organization name] and look forward to hearing from you. If I can provide you with additional information, please let me know. Thank you for your consideration.

GETTING AN OFFER

If you have applied to fifteen organizations, getting an offer can sometimes be tricky. For example, if you hear back first from the organization on the bottom of your list, you may worry that you'll hear back from your top choice just as soon as you accept that less desired position. There's no way around this dilemma; the bottom line is, you can't apply for anything that you wouldn't be thrilled to get. The majority of sponsors are willing to give you a day or so to consider an offer, but you can't expect them to wait much longer. Their resources are limited and when they are ready to make an offer, they want to be able to have the offer accepted so that they can move on to the many other projects on their to-do list. By delaying your response, you're also depriving some other candidate of the opportunity to hear from the sponsor. In someone else's case, that sponsor may be their top choice. If you can, check in with a few of your top choices and let them know you've gotten an offer and you just wanted to find out if they're anywhere near making hiring decisions. Whatever you do, don't accept an offer and then back out of your commitment when you get what you feel is a better offer a month later. Washington is a small place and that sort of unprofessional behavior will be remembered. One student offers very good advice on what to do after you've accepted an offer: "I would also suggest that you get back to the places you applied to when you get another offer. I almost didn't get a job the following year because the sponsor thought they had offered me the position the year before and I had just never responded to their offer. So we had this whole conversation about what happened and it was really unfortunate because I really liked the place and I wish I had known about the offer the year before. So checking in is important, but even checking in after you get another offer might be a good idea."

GETTING TURNED DOWN

You're wondering what I could possibly have to say about not getting a job. You chalk it up to intense competition and you hope something else comes up, right? Mostly, yes. But if it's a place you really had your heart set on and if you are really sure that's a path you want to take, you might consider giving the hiring officer a call and asking her for her thoughts on your application so that you can be better prepared the following year. You never know what will come of it. Consider this story from Michael Bassik:

> I applied to the White House internship and got rejected and I called up the internship director at the White House . . . and I told her who I was and that I had been rejected and then I told her I just felt I was really qualified and I wondered if there was anything she felt I could work on for the next time I applied. So she went through the list and I said, I don't mean to speak out of turn but I really feel like I exude those qualities and I hope they came through in my application and now that you're done with the process maybe you could pull my application and look at it again. Not twenty minutes later she called me back and said what a terrible oversight, we're so sorry, and because they made

this mistake they gave me first choice of the office I wanted to work in and so I got put in the press office. You have to be persistent. It doesn't hurt if you didn't get an internship you applied for to call and ask why and what you could do to be a stronger applicant next time. That alone goes a long way. That might mean that someone might take a second look at your resume, they might send it to someone else whose spots aren't all filled, or maybe they'll keep you in mind for future years, you never know. But be persistent.

A student who shared similar advice found that taking the opportunity to check on an application has been very helpful for future summers:

> I applied at the end of my senior year of high school to my congressman and they said they don't take high schoolers but they encouraged me to apply again the following year. I got the internship the next year. And then this past summer I was applying for a job on the Senate side and I called because I had not heard back from them . . . they said they had filled all their spots, but I used that conversation to talk to the internship coordinator—not being confrontational— about why I didn't get the job, just trying to find out how to be a better candidate, and she said she would put me at the top of the list for the following year.

CHAPTER 5

PRACTICAL ADVICE FOR LIVING AND WORKING IN WASHINGTON

Having found your internship, you may be looking forward to packing your bags and heading off for a great adventure in the nation's capital. Before you do, there are a few things you'll need to figure out. Finding a place to stay and making sure you live reasonably near where you'll be working are worth thinking about well in advance of your departure date. This chapter offers an introduction to Washington and gives you some ideas about things you'll want to do while you're there.

D.C.'S NEIGHBORHOODS

Washington is divided into four quadrants: N.W., N.E., S.W., and S.E. The quadrants radiate out from the Capitol, and you want to be sure you know which quadrant an address is in before you set off to find it, because the very same address can be found in most, if not all, of the four quadrants. Washington is also conveniently laid out on a grid; one way is letters (D Street, S.W., for example) and the other way is numbers. So if you're going to 1401 M Street, N.W., you would head in the direction of 14th Street and M, making sure you're already in N.W. If you need to go to 310 10th Street, N.W., that would be on 10th street between C and D streets (because C is the third letter in the alphabet . . .). The only tricky bit to the grid is the diagonal roads which are named after states; for example, Pennsylvania Avenue, Massachusetts Avenue, and so on. As for the quadrants, they each have their own character and appeal. The next section offers a brief description of the major neighborhoods, running from the Northeast to the Northwest.

Capitol Hill

Starting with the true center of Washington, the Hill has in recent years become an increasingly vibrant community, though post–9/11 there are many more police officers and concrete barriers to negotiate. Living on Capitol Hill means an easy commute to Hill jobs and easy access to many of the tourist sights. You're near Union Station, which is both the Amtrak station and a stop on the Metro system's red line. On the other side of the Capitol Complex is the Capitol South metro stop, on the blue and orange lines. There are plenty of restaurants surrounding the Capitol buildings, and the housing is composed largely of townhomes, particularly as you head east toward Eastern Market. You might find a basement apartment to sublet.

Penn Quarter

Moving toward the Northwest section of Washington you'll head through Penn Quarter. A decade ago, the area to the east of Union Station was a depressing spectacle of half-demolished apartment buildings. The now-named Penn Quarter has been rejuvenated over the past several decades and now boasts museums, theaters, shopping, big flashy restaurants, and contemporary art galleries. Penn Quarter has roughly 10,000 residents, mostly living in new, larger buildings. Penn Quarter has nearly swamped D.C.'s little Chinatown. Surrounding the world's largest single-span Chinese arch at 7th and F Streets, N.W., Chinatown boasts numerous restaurants, the U.S. Mint Museum, the MCI Center, and the annual Chinese New Year's Day parade.

Dupont Circle

If you continue down Massachusetts Avenue, you'll soon come to Dupont Circle, at Connecticut and P Streets, N.W. Dupont is probably the trendiest area in Washington itself, with fashionable restaurants and clubs and lots of young hip people. Kramerbooks & Afterwords is a cultural landmark, having been in the same location since 1976 and known for serving breakfast late into the night. In past decades Dupont was also the hub of the gay scene in Washington, though that has moved a few blocks over to 17th and P Streets, N.W. The housing in Dupont is likely to be the most expensive of the neighborhoods mentioned here. The metro stop is Dupont Circle, on the red line.

Adams Morgan

Adams Morgan has for many years been the more bohemian neighborhood compared to hip, cool Dupont. Moving north from Dupont Circle on 18th Street, Adams Morgan is centered around 18th Street and Columbia Road, N.W. There is a great variety of ethnic restaurants, boutiques, specialty stores, and late-night entertainment. Above and around Adams Morgan there is a large residential neighborhood that has in the past been an affordable alternative, largely because there is no metro stop in Adams Morgan, which means you have to rely on the bus system.

Foggy Bottom

Moving west from Dupont Circle toward Georgetown you'll come to Foggy Bottom, home to the World Bank, the International Monetary Fund, George Washington University (GWU), and the Watergate complex. Many federal government buildings are located here as well. In terms of housing your best bet is the GWU dorms, which we'll talk about later in this chapter. The other advantage of this area is its proximity to the National Mall.

Georgetown

Georgetown is centered on Wisconsin and M Streets, N.W., and is a very popular destination for window shopping and dining. The area features specialty stores, nightclubs, and plenty of restaurants. Of course, Georgetown University is also located here; the disadvantages of living here are the absence of a metro stop and the high rents.

HOUSING IN WASHINGTON

In addition to working for little or no pay, living in Washington means you'll have to pay Washington rental rates. With vacancy rates lower than the national average and demand for short-term housing that explodes over the summer, finding an affordable place to live can be difficult. Finding something near your work might also be tricky. There are basically two options to consider: university dorms and private rentals/sublets.

Dorms in D.C.

Washington is home to several fine universities, including George-town, American, and George Washington. When their students head home for the summer break, all three universities make their dorms available for the thousands of summer interns looking for a place to stay. The advantages of dorms are many; they are air-conditioned (though you'll want to confirm that before signing on the dotted line!), they are furnished, they are already set up to serve a student population (so they'll make moving in and out and everything in between easy), and they are relatively safe. This last point is worth considering; a big, well-lit campus with lots of security measures and a dorm with someone at the front desk 24-7 is probably going to be much safer than renting from a private landlord or subletting and living in a neighborhood that you don't really know and that might not be terribly safe to walk through late at night. If safety tops your list as you're thinking about where to live, you should definitely consider dorm life. As for which university would be best, that will depend upon where you work, but it is most likely that George Washington will be the most convenient. GWU has a metro stop on campus (Foggy Bottom), is near the World Bank, the White House, and many of the agencies, and is a pretty, very safe campus due not only to campus and city police but also added security due to the presence of the World Bank. American's tree-filled campus is certainly less urban than GWU, and it is also less convenient. American is in upper N.W. and their nearest metro stop is Tenleytown, a shuttle bus ride away from campus. American is not near many major employers—it's mostly a residential area—so you're not likely to have a short commute. Georgetown also gets low marks on convenience; there is no metro stop in Georgetown, and you'll have to rely on buses to get across town. If you belong to a fraternity or sorority, you might check to see about vacancies at their houses on George Washington's campus.

LINKS TO UNIVERSITY HOUSING

George Washington University: http://gwired.gwu.edu/gw-
   housing/summerhousing
American University: http://www.american.edu/ocl/housing/
   summer_housing_conferences/intern_housing.html
Georgetown University: http://housing.georgetown.edu/
   summer

Private Rentals

As of spring 2007, Washington's vacancy rate (how many apartments are available to rent) was 3.4 percent, which is about half the
national rate and rivals only New York and Los Angeles. Apartments
are always in high demand in Washington, perhaps because of the
transient nature of Washington's workforce. A change in presidential administrations, for example, results in lots of folks moving out
and a whole different set of people with different political inclinations moving in. While the recent housing slump has resulted in
the conversion of condominiums that had originally been intended
to be sold into rental properties, so far the increase in the number
of rental properties on the market doesn't seem to be affecting average rental rates. The bottom line: expect to pay about $1,000 a
month, particularly if you're going through one of the rental companies. The alternative is to look for a private landlord or a sublet,
which may bring your monthly rent to $600–$800. The trade-offs
are worth considering. Renting from an individual who you don't
know who has a key to your apartment or living with someone you
don't know in a shared apartment may pose safety risks. Or you
could end up renting from an individual who might change their
mind mid-summer, leaving you having to deal with renting hassles
when you should be focusing on your work. Whatever you do (I

can't emphasize this enough), make sure the place you are renting is air-conditioned!

SOURCES FOR PRIVATE RENTALS

Craig's list: http://washingtondc.craigslist.org
The *Washington City Paper*: http://www.washingtoncitypaper.com
The Hill: http://thehill.com

GETTING AROUND

The Metro

The Washington Metro system (http://www.wmata.com) is clean, air-conditioned, and cheap. There are locations near most of the places you'll want to go, and the trains run frequently, particularly at rush hour. Recent increases in ridership have resulted in delays, but particularly if you're living in Washington itself that won't mean much to your commute.

Bicycles

As a former bicycle courier in Washington, I can vouch for the convenience of commuting by bicycle in what really is quite a small town. However, there are several downsides worth considering. First, unless it's two blocks and downhill both ways you're going to get very hot and sweaty, which may not be the look you're going for professionally. Second, there is heavy traffic congestion in Washington, which makes being on a bicycle on those streets potentially dangerous. Third, if you plan on cycling, carry a big lock and be careful where you leave your bike; bike thieves are rampant.

Cars

If you have lived your life in the suburbs and are accustomed to driving everywhere, spending your summer in Washington is your chance to give the environment a break. Bringing your car to D.C. is just asking for trouble. Traffic is terrible, parking is worse, and broken windows are common in some neighborhoods. If you can, plan on using public transportation.

TOURISM TIPS

There are plenty of tourism guides to Washington (*Lonely Planet*, *Eyewitness Travel*, *Unofficial Guide*, etc.) and I strongly suggest you have a look at a few of these and maybe even buy one of them for your time in Washington. In addition to spending many lovely Saturday mornings on the Mall (the National Mall is a two-mile expanse lined by the Smithsonian museums, bookended by the Capitol on the eastern end and the Washington Monument on the western end, with the reflecting pool running down the middle), you may also spend some weekend time at Arlington Cemetery, the wonderful zoo, breakfasting at Eastern Market (on Capitol Hill), or enjoying some of the off-the-Mall museums. You should also consider taking some of the excellent tours that are available. If you are (understandably) put off by the idea of waiting in really long lines on hot sweltering days, know that your Member of Congress can arrange VIP tours where lines are much shorter and the tours are longer and more informative. Here's how to do it: as soon as you know you'll be in D.C. for the summer, you should check the website for your Member of Congress. (To figure out who your Member of Congress and Senators are, go to http://www.vote-smart.org and enter your ZIP code. If you already know who your Member of Congress is, you can go to http://www.house.gov and use the dropdown menu to reach your Member's site.) Most (but not all) of their websites have a link that says something like "visiting Washington," or you may need to look under "constituent services" for tour requests. If that fails, give the office a call. The number of tours they offer and when they start taking requests varies widely, as does their ability to honor all requests. Members of Congress who represent districts near Washington get deluged by requests, while Members from far-off places have more tickets available to give away and may be eager to offer more personalized service. Also check your Senators' websites to find out what tours they facilitate.

To get you started, here's a list of ten must-dos:

1. U.S. Capitol Tour: This tour is usually provided either directly or indirectly by your congressional office. They can arrange for tickets for you to take the official tour, or one of their staff (or more likely one of their interns) can take you on the tour. Make sure you take time after the tour to sit in the galleries. The galleries of the Senate and House of Representatives are open to view whenever either body is in session. The House gallery is also open Monday–Friday, 9:00 a.m. to 4:00 p.m. when the House is not in session, though that's pretty boring as you're looking down at an empty room. The Senate gallery is not open if the Senate is not in session. Gallery passes, different for each chamber, are obtained from the office of your Senator or Representative and are required to enter the gallery whether they are in session or not. This gives you an opportunity to stop by your Member's office to say hello!

2. Congressional Hearings: Take at least one opportunity to sit in on a congressional hearing. They are listed daily in the *Washington Post* (Section A) and you can also find hearing

schedules in *Congress Daily* (http://nationaljournal.com/about/congressdaily) in the Daybook. If you want a little more notice, you could also browse the committees (from dropdown menu on http://www.house.gov or http://senate.gov) and check their hearing schedule. No reservations or special pass is required to attend a hearing, though the more popular or controversial topics might fill the room, so in those cases you might want to arrive early. If you do turn up early to a hearing on, say, tax policy and the line is made up of people who look like they don't really care about tax policy, possibly because they don't pay taxes, they're just holding spots for those high-paid lobbyists we talked about earlier. Read *Showdown at Gucci Gulch* for more on lobbyists who can pay for people to wait in line for them.

3. U.S. Department of State Diplomatic Reception Rooms: If you have an interest in diplomacy, a visit to the State Department is right up your alley. While this is not an "operations" tour, it does get you in the door and allows you to see some of the rooms where high-level diplomacy happens. For reservations (required, and recommended 90 days in advance), go to http://receptiontours.state.gov but check with your Member first—if you don't see this tour on their list, ask if they can arrange it for you.

4. Supreme Court: Half-hour guided tours take you into the stunning courtroom and provide an overview of the work of the Court. Unfortunately, you won't likely be around for an oral argument, which happen October through April, though the Court is still in session through June. If you're interested in law, this is definitely worth a visit. This tour is typically arranged by your congressional office.

5. National Archives: The main building on Constitution Av-

enue (between 7th and 9th Streets, N.W.) houses the Declaration of Independence, the Constitution, and the Bill of Rights. Reservations can be made (at least six weeks in advance) at visitorservices@nara.gov or through your Member of Congress, though you can typically walk right in with no wait if you time it right.

6. White House: Of course, no summer in Washington would be complete without a visit to the White House. Post-9/11, the tour is available only through your Member of Congress or Senator, you need to schedule it three to six months in advance, and it is a somewhat limited tour. But, hey, you get to go into the White House!

7. Library of Congress: Frankly, the Library makes the top ten list because I happen to have a thing for libraries. Others may enjoy the tour for other reasons; the recently reopened Jefferson Building (closed since 1984) houses, among other things, a rough draft by Jefferson of the Declaration of Independence and Lincoln's early drafts of the Gettysburg Address. The main reading room is lovely, and it's worth flashing you driver's license and requesting a book just to sit there and read. Most congressional offices have tickets for this tour; otherwise, you'll have to join the public tour line early in the morning to pick up a ticket for a tour later in the day.

8. The final three on the list are very interesting media tours in lieu of the expensive Newseum (opened summer 2008). The first is the Voice of America (VOA). The VOA, funded by the U.S. government, broadcasts internationally more than 1,000 hours of news, information, educational, and cultural programming every week to an estimated worldwide audience of more than 115 million people. The tour

takes you through many of their recording studios, where
you can see and hear actual broadcasts being recorded in
many languages. They have an online ticketing system at
http://ibb7.ibb.gov/voatickets/index.cfm.

9. National Public Radio leads tours of its broadcast facilities
every Thursday at 11 A.M. Call four weeks ahead to reserve
a spot (202/513-3232).

10. Tours of the *Washington Post* are conducted on Monday
from 10 A.M to 3 P.M; reservations are taken four weeks in
advance. Tours of the *Post*'s printing plants are also available
(202/334-7969).

SAFETY AND HEALTH

Just a few things you may want to do before packing your bags.
While it is very unlikely that you should fall ill, have an accident, or
be in Washington when there is a terrorist attack, you probably want
to think a bit about what you would do if something like that were
to happen. First, make sure you have health insurance coverage and
you bring your identification card with you, and carry it with you at
all times. Know where the hospital is (George Washington University Hospital in Foggy Bottom is probably your best bet), and think
about who you can call for help if you are sick or injured while in
D.C. This may be another intern, who may also need an emergency
buddy. Also think about how your friends or family would reach you
in case of emergency, such as some sort of disaster or attack. Consider making a phone tree so that you have to call only one person
outside of Washington to tell them that you're safe, where you are,
and what you are going to do, and then they can make some calls for
you. There is also a service offered by the D.C. government called

Alert D.C.; they send out emergency notices via email or text messaging. The messages I typically get are about road closures and bad weather, but they are prepared to handle much worse. The website to register is https://textalert.ema.dc.gov/index.php?CCheck=1.

CHAPTER 6

TACTICAL ADVICE: HOW TO BE A GREAT INTERN

This chapter offers plenty of advice on being successful in your internship. One thing you should remember is that the work of Washington is fueled in large part by the labor of interns. While there may be some supervisors who see you as just free labor and who don't intend to mentor you or help you find a job after you graduate, they are in the minority and you will have avoided them because you asked all the right questions during your interview. Most employers really do value your contribution; Liz Conroy in Senator Casey's office says, "We just have to have our office running and we could not do that without interns. From the front desk to tours to getting constituent letters answered—we could not do all that without interns." Interviews also suggest that sponsors really do want you to have a good experience and want to help you navigate Washington. Given your sponsor's desire to see you succeed, this chapter focuses on the things you need to remember to do, the attitude you need to have, the questions you need to ask, and a few things you should really not do. Student tips and advice from internship sponsors are particularly useful in this chapter, which focuses on getting the most from Washington and the internship experience. How to communicate with your supervisor, what to expect, and how to get interesting assignments are also covered. First we'll address what to wear in this conservative town with its swamp-like summers.

WASHINGTON FASHION: ZOMBIE CHIC

Washington fashion—now that's an oxymoron. Washington is a town of conservative dressers, a sea of dark suits and muted ties. Why, you wonder, is the D.C. dress code so dull? I have my theories. First, there is the matter of government salaries. In 2007, Members of Congress had an annual salary of $165,000. This may sound like a nice chunk of change to a college student living on somewhere around $20,000 a year, but consider that Members typically need to have a house in their home district and a place to stay in the Washington metro area, where the median house/condo price in 2006 was $419,000. The average Chief of Staff in Congress makes about $100,000 and the average Legislative Correspondent makes a whopping $25,000 a year. Even if you're sharing your efficiency with three people and eating lots of ramen noodles, there's not going to be much left for the latest fashion must-haves. Of course, there are lots of people who earn lots of money in Washington, mostly in the private sector. In addition to not wanting to out-dress the people they're asking favors of, they may not want to flaunt just how much money they're making by getting Members of Congress to do nice things for their clients.

Second, if in fact you do manage to have some room in your budget and a desire to shop, there is a risk that you are making the wrong statement about your priorities in workaholic Washington.

Fashionable people, it may be assumed, are spending too much time in their closets or at the mall and not enough time at their desks. In fact, I think the look many in D.C. strive for is zombie chic. I witnessed this firsthand some years ago; I was at a meeting of legislative directors who were being briefed by the senior staff of the House leadership on an upcoming bill. These are the people who work for the Speaker and others in leadership positions in the House—Very Important People. As they filed in through a door at the front of the room, my first thought was, these people need some sleep. They all had bags under their eyes, frizzy hair, wrinkled shirts, and very serious looks on their obviously tired faces. And these were the movers and shakers! So if you looked like them, you clearly were working long hours doing very important things for very important people. On the other hand, if you waltz into a meeting with a sassy wraparound silky dress number and pointy high heels, you may be shooting yourself in the (tottering) foot.

The bottom line is (and this is of course true outside of Washington too), your clothes send a message. As one student says, "I really tried to impress the people in my office. I wore a suit every day, I wore very muted colors . . . I was very serious about my work—I wanted them to know I was capable and ready for full-time work." If you want to be taken seriously, you have to look the part.

What to Wear

Having established that you don't want to stand out in the crowd at least as far as your attire goes, we'll turn now to dress expectations in various parts of working Washington. Starting with the most formal, if you are interning in the Senate or at a large lobbying firm, you've got to dress up. Most, if not all, of these employers expect coat and tie on men and similarly appropriate dress for women. For men, this means investing in one or two suits, one or two versatile sports coats, and at least three pairs of good summer-weight suit pants (not casual!). For women, suits (pant or skirt) are a good way to go, but you can often get away with nice pants/skirt and a blouse. On the subject of shoes, one student makes a small but useful suggestion: "Don't wear high heels if you're working on Capitol Hill. And don't wear shoes that flap or go click-click as you walk down the halls." When you get to Washington, you'll soon understand why she flung her mules to the back of her closet after a day of wearing them at work. Particularly in the House and Senate, the hallways are wide and most are marble. What this means is that unlike in an office building with carpeted hallways, your clack-clack echoes everywhere and just takes something away from your very serious, here-to-save-the-world attitude.

Liz Conroy in Senator Casey's office says there is a clear dress code and anything less may pose a problem for you: "Our dress code is business/professional while we're in session and business/casual while we're in recess but in either case you have to remember you're still representing us. We've definitely had a few cases of girls in sundresses and skimpy tank tops and we had to send them home. You're representing a Senator so you really need to think about that."

I WISH I HAD KNOWN...

". . . how formal to dress. It's sometimes hard to figure out on the Senate side. They'll tell you you're supposed to wear a suit but then you get there and all the staff are in jeans and you're in a suit. The policy in my office was when the Senator was in you wear a suit and when he was out (in the District) you could wear jeans but the interns are often not told when the Senator would be in or out so we often turned up in suits when everyone else was in jeans—I think the staff thought that was a little funny sometimes—it was kind of like a hazing thing initially. After a while they would clue us in."

At the smallest of nonprofits, more casual attire might be perfectly fine. On your first day, regardless of where you're going, dress like you're going on a job interview. For most of you, this is the first time you'll be meeting your sponsor, and you want to send the right message. Some extra tips are in order here:

- Even if you dress casually, make it business casual and conservative; no shorts, no flip-flops, no vast expanses of exposed skin. D.C. is very conservative as dress goes, and you want to fit in. Wondering how conservative is conservative enough? One internship sponsor who started life in Washington as an intern offers a cautionary tale:

> You don't want to stand out too much in the way you dress. I remember I wore funky socks—it didn't really go over well. . . . I think the first thing you learn coming to an office is cologne/perfume has no place in the workplace and that's something that students are not used to because when they get dressed up they're generally going out and that might mean adding a splash of cologne. It's a terrible professional faux pas and I will admit to not hiring individuals with overwhelming scents. . . . In the Clinton White House I was an intern in the press office and my boss asked to borrow my tie because he hadn't worn a tie that day and happened to be pulled into a meeting and needed a tie. I was not wearing cologne but the last time I had worn that tie I had cologne on and after the meeting was

over he came to me and said, "you should have told me your tie had cologne on it because I wouldn't have worn it."

- D.C. is very humid and very hot in the summer. Wear cotton or breathable synthetics. Advice for women: pants and pant suits may be the better option if you're working somewhere that expects nylons when you're wearing a skirt (and many places apart from the smaller advocacy groups do!).
- If you attend any speaking engagements or events put on by your university or some other group, be sure to dress properly. There's an embarrassing photo of a group from a university who went to the White House and had a photo with the President, and some of the students were dressed in flip-flops and shorts. This is, of course, very disrespectful to the person you're meeting and sends the wrong message about why you're in D.C.

Another tricky part about dress code is that you can't always follow the example set by staff. In some cases that's because (particularly younger) staff aren't really setting a very good example. In other cases, more senior staff or research staff may be able to follow a different (unspoken) dress code than other staff can follow. Either way, you're better off trying to send the message that you're serious. Advice from Erin Green at the Center for American Progress: "Dress code is a big one for me. Flip-flops drive me crazy. Ripped jeans—I just want to make it very clear at the beginning. And it's hard because this is their first time in an office environment and then they look at how staff are dressed and they think it's ok to wear very casual clothes and it's really not." If you have any doubt about the dress code and you don't want to go to the trouble and expense of putting together a formal wardrobe if you don't have to, ask your internship coordinator when you call them back to accept the offer. They'll appreciate that you asked. Finally, if you've gone to the trouble of buying nice business clothes, if your sleeves or pant legs are too long, see a tailor.

THE DOS AND DON'TS OF THE D.C. DRESS CODE

Rules for Men	Rules for Women
Neat, short haircuts	Hair pulled back
No facial hair	Subtle jewelry—nothing dangling
Conservative tie	No revealing tops
Business pants/shirts	Skirts no higher than an inch or so above the knee (if that)
No sneakers	Pantyhose, skin color
No shorts	No shorts

MIND YOUR MANNERS

If this is your first experience in an office environment, there may be a few things that you'll find challenging. In addition to dressing the part, you need to be polite and fairly formal all the time. You should in most ways behave like a full-time employee, rather than a guest. Keep your workplace neat, particularly if it is shared. Also be responsible when using communal spaces: "General workplace etiquette is also important and sometimes they don't realize that they're expected to refill the copier if they use up the paper or clean up a workspace where they've been working" (Erin Green, Center for American Progress).

Once you get comfortable in an office and start to make some friends, you may run the risk of getting a little too comfortable. Remember that in most cases you are very visible; offices are shared or communal and people are busy doing their own work and don't want to be interrupted or distracted by loud talking or laughter. You also need to remember that you are representing your office: "In the front office, interns get a little casual and joking and putting their feet up and so on but you need to remember that this is the front of Senator Casey's office—this is the first perception that people get of him and how the office runs so up here you really need to conduct yourself professionally" (Liz Conroy, Senator Casey's office).

OFFICE HOURS

You also may find it difficult to get used to the daily grind, which is even tougher in Washington, where hours are long. Be sure to know on your first day (and preferably before then) what your office hours will be. While you may not be comfortable asking these kinds of questions during your interview, once you get the offer you should feel free to ask about office hours, dress code, security procedures, and anything else you're wondering about. Be sure to ask about hours, because this is something that varies widely in Washington, and you don't want to be surprised by what's expected. Neither of the following two students knew what their office hours were going to be before starting and found very different expectations in their workplaces:

> I had to come in at 8:30 and leave at 5:30 and if we were five minutes late, they would send us home. We had 45 minutes for lunch and that included getting around the Pentagon, which is big and difficult to get around. It was unbelievably strict. I guess that's part of the experience being in the Pentagon. (college junior)

My office was very flexible, especially when the Secretary
was not in. When he was traveling, my supervisor would
tell me I could come in a little later. There were some nights
I would stay until seven if there was something that had to
be finished, but a lot of times at around 3:00 they would
say, you're an intern, you should go do something interesting outside of this office. So it just varied from day to day.
One thing that surprised me is you would get 20 minutes
for lunch; you were expected to go get your lunch and come
back to the office. But I appreciated that they let me do
things outside of the office. (college senior)

Sponsors tell me that in order to assign you the more interesting projects, they need to know that you're going to be there every
day for at least six and preferably eight or ten weeks. Sponsors understand your need to have experiences outside of your internship;
show up early and keep a regular schedule and they won't mind
if you leave early for events like speakers or hearings, as long as it
doesn't get it the way of your work and you don't overdo it. In addition to being an easy way to show your enthusiasm about your
internship, one student on the Senate side points out another more
practical advantage to being the first in the office:

In the Senate there are a lot of briefings and interns are often
asked to go to them and there are a range of briefings, some
are interesting and some aren't. So there was a lot of competition to get the better briefings. But the thing is there was a
sign-up sheet every day for the briefings so people who got
to the office earlier got the better ones and I was amazed at
how many people didn't show up a few minutes early but
then complained about never getting the good briefings. It's

really important to be prompt and even come a few minutes early to make yourself available to people.

While in most cases coming in early means sometime after eight and before nine, there are places where being treated like staff may mean doing interesting work but it may also mean getting up really, really early: "The internship I did was right after I graduated and I was still used to my college schedule which of course is very flexible. My internship was at the Department of Defense and everyone in that office would get in at 6:00 or 6:30 in the morning and it was just brutal. They actually let me come in a little later, at 7:00 in the morning because I was an intern and getting paid a little less than everyone else but it was a tough adjustment" (college graduate).

Finally, when you get to your internship you may find that staff don't take lunch and might be a little impatient with you if you expect to. If you're in the House or Senate (and lots of other places in D.C.), there isn't really a lunch hour. House staff, for example, regularly grab food from the cafeteria and then go back to their offices, where their lunches sit for an hour or two before they have a chance to eat. While this varies by organization, you probably shouldn't expect to be out of the office every day for a relaxing lunch hour.

ASKING FOR WORK

On your first day, you may get a full tour of your sponsoring organization followed by a detailed description of your work duties, or you may be shown to a desk and be told to await further instructions, which may not come for hours or days. Either way, take it in stride and stay positive. When introduced, try to remember people's names, and use their names when you speak to them. That may prompt them to remember your name, which is the first step to getting interesting assignments. Stay positive and don't worry, the work will come. While you're sitting around waiting for that exciting project, read the dailies—*The Hill*, *Roll Call*, and of course the *Washington Post* (and don't spend your time looking at Facebook). Here's some advice on waiting and asking for work: "I really struggled the first few days because they didn't have anything for me to do and it was horrible but then on the fourth day I asked this staffer if I could do anything at all for her and she handed me this speech she was just starting to write and she asked me to proofread it and I did and reworked it and now it's her standard stump speech and even now she emails me when she uses it. So it's just really important to ask for work and to do it well."

When the work does come, make sure you do it in the order they want it done, not most interesting first. Do the easy/boring/clerical projects right so that you can move on to the more interesting work. One student offered good advice on this front: "If you're getting a mix of tasks, you might want to ask which ones are the priority. Of course you don't want offend your supervisor but a lot of times they'll tell you to do this and this and if you don't get to that project until next week that's fine. I think most of us have worked for people who are not much older than us and so they are sympathetic and they know we want to do the more interesting work so if you get that permission to do the more interesting project first, that's fine as long as you make sure you do everything they want when they want it."

The internship experience varies widely, and the type of work you do and how you get your assignments are no exception. In some cases, your internship sponsor will have very clear tasks set out for you and how you do them will be thoroughly explained. In other cases, you may have to be more proactive about getting work assignments. In either case, remember that starting with your first assignment, your work product is being evaluated. The better your work product is, the more likely you are to get an even more interesting assignment next time. The first assignments are an important opportunity to establish how capable you are: "Just a couple weeks in, one of our clients had a big event we were putting together for them, and it involved putting briefing books together and setting up meetings with Members of Congress and for the lobbyists on the project—my supervisors—to see that I could be counted on to accomplish these tasks really set the stage for the second half of the internship in terms of what they expected of us and it was a way of sending the message to them that they could trust me with more advanced work" (college junior).

Your first assignments are also a good way for you to start establishing relationships and creating opportunities to network, and often it's essential that you take the initiative. Chris Andresen at Dutko Group explains:

> When you come in here, it's kind of like university. We assign you to a specific practice area or issue and the reality is if you want to sit at your desk and not do a lot of work and kind of go unnoticed, you might be able to get away with that. Most of the time fortunately people don't want to do that. They want to get involved and they want to know people and take on more work than they're assigned. The internships that haven't worked out are the people that stay to themselves, they don't get to meet the other officers here, they don't get to meet the assistants and associates who are not much older than the interns and have similar goals.

Liz Conroy in Senator Casey's office relates a similar experience working in the Senator's office:

The work is typically half administrative and half legislative work which still may be mundane stuff but it should be legislatively geared. But you need to be proactive about that. If you're sitting around and the LCs and LAs are really busy, unless you make yourself known, other projects are not going to happen. The people in the office who have volunteered to work with you have done so because they think they can be a good mentor to interns and they want to work with you but you really need to be proactive....We have had everyone from someone who when he was hired to intern we thought he would be great and he ended up spending the entire time in the mail room and wasn't even productive with data entry, which can be a stepping stone to getting at least a little more interesting work, to someone who goes through their data entry, gets tons done every day and has attended committee hearings, written memos to the Senator, gone on trips for the LA—it all depends how much you're willing to put into it and then your legislative mentor will trust you and depend on you to produce and that's all incredibly important to your experience. People need to know coming in here that we'll show you the ropes, we'll show you what's out there but you need to be proactive.

One benefit of an internship in D.C. for many students was to learn how to ask for work and to gain the confidence to ask people who look very busy and important to take the time to come up with an interesting assignment for you. One student shares her experience:

In my office I learned to be confident and ask if I wanted to work on a project or tell them there was a particular topic

I wanted to write on and so it taught me to not be afraid
to ask to be involved in projects because it turned out the
staff really appreciated that and I think at first they're kind
of afraid to give you a lot of work because they don't know
what the quality of your work is and they're on really tight
deadlines, so if you put yourself out there and assuming
you do a good job you build your own confidence and they
build their confidence in you and will really rely on you as
a member of the staff and will give you a lot of work to do.
(college senior)

In addition to knowing how and when to ask for work, it is essential that you do the assignments well, which means you need to
be clear on how exactly the project needs to be done. One student
who learned this lesson the hard way says, "When you get assigned
a project, ask lots of questions about what they want because that's
better than turning in an assignment that was not what they wanted"
(college junior). Another student had similar stumbles at first: "It's
very important to keep in mind what they want—not just what they
want but how they want it. In the beginning I would give them a
completed project and they would send it back because there was
something I didn't do that they assumed I would know to do so I
guess it would have been better if I had asked lots of questions up
front." Another student figured it out, but observed the fate of a less
successful student:

You've got to ask a lot of questions. You're coming in and
getting assignments that they actually have pretty specific
ideas about—things like formatting were very important.
There was a very specific way, for example, to lay out an
Excel spreadsheet. And not doing it the right way means

the person who assigned it to you has to go back and do it
and my experience this past summer, there was another intern who really didn't appreciate how important it is to use
the format they want rather than the format or style that you
think works better. I think he was really penalized for that in
the other work he got down the road. (college junior)

Given that this is pressure-cooker Washington, you may find
that your supervisor just doesn't have time for your first question,
much less your sixth clarifying question: "I had a moment that re-
minded me of *Devil Wears Prada*. I went to ask a question about an
assignment—they had asked me to put together a handout and my
boss just said, 'figure it out.' I was on deadline, I had no idea what
I was doing and I had to figure it out without bothering anyone"
(college junior). In those cases, consider it an opportunity to show
them your impressive ability to work independently and hope for
the best. In most cases, however, staff don't want to have to cor-
rect mistakes that could have been easily explained at the outset, so
you're likely to get reasonably good guidance, as long as they know
you need it. So you have to ask!

Once you prove yourself, you may have some flexibility when
it comes to choosing projects. While that won't be true in all cases,
this student's experience shows that while you need to do some of
the administrative work, the busier you are with interesting projects
(and assuming you do a good job on those), the less you'll be doing
boring projects:

I worked over the summer at PBS and it was a really small
office and I was brought on to work with everyone. So you
could work with the producers who just wanted me to
come up with story ideas and research them, find places

to shoot, and really gave me a lot of creative responsibility. The person in the cube next to me was the tape librarian and he was a nice guy and whenever he needed help he would ask me and of course there are a lot of tapes. So if I didn't have anything that I was working on that I chose to work on, then I would have to do the more menial tapes. So while you of course want to say yes to the menial tasks because that's how you build good relationships, you also want to think about and find projects that are closer to your own interests. (college senior)

You can also turn a boring task into an opportunity to get assigned better projects: "On the Hill you're one of many interns and so maybe you'll get an assignment that's not the best thing in the world—when I was working on the Hill I was asked to go to a hearing that frankly no one was really interested in and I went and came back and did a kind of funny one-pager, just bullets with a three-line intro at the top and the person I did it for loved it and sent me to a lot more hearings after that and let me do more important projects" (college junior). Also, as has been said elsewhere, the boring projects are the way to more interesting projects. This student didn't have to figure that out for herself: "I think I got bribed for an assignment once. They asked me to do this really boring but complicated spreadsheet of airplane arrivals and departures between Washington and our district, and the guy who assigned it to me said if I did a good job with it he would give me something more interesting. So after I finished that project, I got to do research on the immigration issue, which was really interesting, and the Senator was really involved and so it was exciting to have been part of that" (college junior).

DON'T BE A STAR STALKER!

"I'll tell you one of the big don'ts that come up frequently—let's call them 'Star-Stalker Interns' who either sit outside of Hillary Clinton's office or they wait outside the [Capitol] subway, just waiting to see who will get off and get an autograph . . . we will have not only other Senators but we had two movie stars last summer who came up to the Hill to talk about Uganda and our interns were standing outside the door gawking and it just made our office look unprofessional. So while we will try and expose you to as many people as we can, and you will be able to see people in the halls and in hearings, you can't stalk people, it's just not professional and it reflects badly on our office." (Liz Conroy at Senator Casey's office)

"When you're working in government for an elected official, the role of the intern is really to be a fly on the wall and not to be too star struck. You'll have opportunities to meet people but you need to blend in. I learned that lesson the hard way in the White House—there are times for shaking people's hands and taking pictures and there are times to just get on with the work." (Michael Bassik, MSHC Partners)

Ask for projects but don't pester. If you have ideas, suggest them when you're told there's no work for you to do, but don't expect an immediate response. If you've really got nothing to do, find a relevant congressional hearing to attend—your sponsor will like your initiative and it will get you out of the office.

FIND A NICHE

Notwithstanding the many times and different ways in this book that the internship sponsors I interviewed have said how important it is to be happy doing the little boring jobs, students and sponsors alike find that it's very useful to find a particular issue that you focus at least part of your time on. Michael Bassik has this advice:

> If you're on Capitol Hill and you do an internship, you're one of a whole lot of people who will come out with the exact same skills so it's really helpful to specialize. So for example, you might decide to take an interest in health care policy and write a memo on health care policy and get to talk to the Member of Congress about the issue. That way when you're done with your internship and you're interviewing for your next internship there is a particular thing that you can talk about and it differentiates you. And then you become known as a person who has this expertise and maybe you end up being a resource.

I WISH I HAD KNOWN ...

"This past summer there was a lot of flexibility for interns. If you had something specific about Iraq that you were interested in and that you had studied, it's such a big topic in general that if you had some insight or some expertise or passion about one aspect they were more than willing to let you go off and work on that if they didn't have you tasked to something else. I think in lots of these places, rather than having you play solitaire when you didn't have anything to do, but you had something relevant to work on, they're more than willing to let you do that and a lot of times that will turn out to be useful to them. So it's really important when you come in with an idea of what you can do on the side—it took me a week or two to figure that out and I wish I had known coming in what project I could do because I could have produced even more" (college senior).

Another student has similar advice: "I felt [what was] important was finding something you really care about and really learn about it so that when this issue comes up you have something to talk about and tell your boss that you're really interested in. I told my boss that I was really interested in this one aspect of legislation and he allowed me to write a paper about it" (college senior). Another student suggests that even when you haven't quite graduated from grunt work, you can try to target your grunt projects so that they lead to substantive projects; "I think that while you should always ask for work, be smart about who you ask. In the Senate the staff are divided by issue area and since my interest was health policy I made sure to ask that staffer for work whenever I could" (college junior).

GETTING FEEDBACK

Like asking for work, once you turn in a project you might not know when an appropriate time is to ask what they thought about your project or what you might have done better. You might not have to worry, as many supervisors will be proactive about giving feedback so that you can do a better job with the next assignment. However, some supervisors may be working on multiple projects and may not get around to reviewing your product for some time. In that case, you may need to observe what's going on and make yourself visible to the person who assigned you to the project, but don't expect immediate comments. Keep busy with other assignments and, if after a few days (or more) you still haven't heard back, you might just want to send a quick email (or whatever the appropriate method of communication is in your office) asking if there was anything else on the project you can do. The following advice may also help: "Sometimes interns expect if they hand in a paper that they're going to get feedback immediately but everyone is so busy here that they need to know they're going to have to wait. It's actually a lot of work to have interns on top of everything else and while of course interns can take some of the workload, mentoring and training adds to the workload and so interns need to be aware of what they're asking and when they're asking" (Erin Green, Center for American Progress).

OFFICE ROMANCE: DON'T DO IT!

Monica Lewinsky was not the first intern to do something really embarrassing and inappropriate during her Washington stay and, sadly, she will not be the last. My comments are relevant for both men and women, though unfortunately men get away with all kinds of stuff a woman never could, so women should pay particular attention. There are so many reasons to avoid anything approaching sex with your officemates or employer, I don't know where to start. Here are two points to consider:

1. Do you really want to be the fresh meat? Interviews for an article in *The Hill* suggest that many (male) staffers and lobbyists look forward to the summer crop of interns, and not just because they'll get help with their filing. Not cool.
2. The women staffers won't like it. Dressing inappropriately and in-office flirtations are particularly frowned upon by the women on staff, who feel that sort of behavior demeans all women and undermines their efforts to be taken seriously. If you choose the interns-gone-wild summer path, don't expect a particularly flattering letter of recommendation from your female Chief of Staff.

If you don't want to take my word for it, a number of the people I interviewed agreed wholeheartedly with my position, including Michael Bassik: "There's no good that can come of it. There's no positive aspect for the employer or the intern. It really does create an awkward working environment and it can hurt your future job prospects. The intern might think this person they've had a relationship with would be a good person to be an advocate for them but that person might then feel awkward about being an advocate."

This chapter has focused on how to impress your internship sponsor and how to have a substantive and successful internship experience. In the next chapter I will talk about what you can do to make sure the good work you did will not be forgotten. I will also address how to go about keeping in touch with people in Washington so that when it comes time for your next internship or your first job, you'll have a network to reach out to.

CHAPTER 7

USING THE INTERNSHIP TO PROPEL YOUR CAREER

As Washingtonians know, they live and work in a small town where networking is the key to career advancement. Students new to Washington will benefit from taking full advantage of networking to prepare for their careers. Tips on making contacts and keeping them, how to network, and what to expect from the networking process are included in this chapter.

THE BENEFITS OF A D.C. INTERNSHIP

Earlier chapters abound with stories from students and sponsors about the benefits of an internship in Washington. Students acquire research skills, content area experience, and ideas about where they want their career paths to go. You also will have had an opportunity to make an impression on some really important people. Liz Conroy in Senator Casey's office speaks to their willingness to help good interns find jobs: "There are going to be some interns who you are going to be willing to stick your neck out for. . . . we had one guy last summer who was just a fantastic intern and now he's back looking for a job and there are a couple people in the office who have been making calls for him and setting up appointments—if they were an amazing intern we will go to bat for them."

But what if your experience was not all that you had hoped or what if you decided that politics is not where you want to be? Was your summer wasted? Chris Andresen, who is very happy working in Washington, suggests that ruling out this career path is just as useful as ruling it in: "I think that an internship in D.C.—at least for me it reassured me—I wasn't completely sold on coming to D.C. but the internship sparked my interest in coming to D.C. It can also do the opposite—if you come here and you don't like it, you know that you probably won't be back in D.C. and that's valuable too."

If you decide after spending a summer or semester in D.C. that you want to come back after you graduate, all the internship sponsors I spoke to said that having had a Washington internship is very helpful for job candidates. According to Chris Andresen: "Having an internship on your resume—whether on the congressional side or the lobbying side—when you're ready to come back to Washington, it advances you a little bit past the entry-level folks who might be coming to D.C. with no real experience. When you're in D.C., it's kind of a different mindset and it gives you a different perspective from someone coming in with no D.C. experience." In fact, in recent years the internship has become the first rung on the career ladder as opposed to an optional plus for your resume; before getting the receptionist or legislative correspondent position, the expectation is that you'll have done an internship on the Hill.

Several students and sponsors talked about the value of doing multiple internships: "Some of our younger interns really get an even bigger jump because then the following year they get an even

more prestigious internship because someone here knows someone
that can help" (Chris Andresen, Dutko Group). In addition to the
value of the Washington experience generally, the research skills that
are acquired on the job in Washington are recognized to be invaluable when you move on to your next internship or job.

> In terms of skills that interns obtain during an internship,
> . . . writing skills. . . . we'll ask an intern to go to a hearing
> and then prepare a memo for a client on what was said. It's
> a good skill to have that you get through this internship is
> you're taking a lot of information and condensing it. It's the
> opposite of what you are asked to do in school and it's so
> important in Washington to be able to take a complex topic
> and condense it down to a one-pager (Chris Andresen,
> Dutko Group).

> I spent a lot of time writing in my internship and I found
> out that research skills are really important. The research
> skills that I learned through my internship overshadowed
> anything I learned in coursework. In terms of depth of
> research and pulling together so much material and then
> trying to write and summarize something. Research skills
> are very important—being able to take a lot of information
> and synthesize it into something that everybody can under-
> stand. (college junior)

> For my internship I had to do a couple of background
> guides on issues. For example, the Senator wanted to know
> about the Armenian genocide so I had to summarize this
> huge issue into a page or two. So research skills are very
> important and I think that's probably true in lots of differ-

ent internships in Washington because often it's the interns who take the first stab at a research project so that staff can then decide what they want to do on the issue. (college junior)

I was working for a lobbyist and I did a lot of research but the other part of that is it had to be done quickly. Time frames are very short and you have to be able to turn around projects very quickly. (college senior)

On a more practical but no less important level, I was pleased to hear from a number of students that their internship supervisors were willing to review resumes and suggest improvements. Two interns relate their resume clean-up stories:

Once I was at my internship I sat down with my supervisors and asked them to review my resume and they edited it and ended up giving it to one of their secretaries who completely reformatted it for me and they produced this beautiful resume and gave me lots of useful advice on the application process and so I think talking to people once you get a job about how to make your materials better for the future can be really useful. (college senior)

My boss at the State Department looked at my resume and he took a red pen to it and made all kinds of changes and it was so helpful. I'm so glad I took advantage of that opportunity to ask these people who actually do the hiring in the field I'm interested in to review my resume and help me get it right. (college senior)

MAKING A GOOD IMPRESSION

Enthusiasm, you may recall, is an important thing to have during a job interview. It's also important to carry that over to the day-to-day work once you get there. This point has been made elsewhere in the book, but more than anything on your resume, your attitude will determine your success in Washington. One perceptive student says, "It's more than being hardworking, it seems like it's really important in Washington to be passionate about the work."

> I think you've just got to be supermotivated. You've got to be ready and willing to outwork the other interns and you've got to make the most of your time here because in the end it's very valuable to you. Because in your next interview for an internship or a job they're going to say, "So what about your internship last summer" and if you didn't really get anything out of it, that's not really interesting. So for the future, it's really important just to stay motivated and always to be looking for more work. And you've got to be willing to do the small things, the office tasks, and just stay really positive. (Chris Andresen, Dutko Group)

Internship sponsors and the mentors at work to whom you are assigned not only are glad to have administrative help but also are eager to help you further your career. When they go out of their way to help you, be warned that they may get offended if you don't participate or appreciate what they're doing. An example from Erin Green at the Center for American Progress:

> I think it's important to take advantage of everything while you're here. Don't just get sucked into that one research

project. Try to meet people and talk to people, go to the events that are offered. For example, we do brown bags once a week with staff; interns should take advantage of that. We had a morning event last year—I had John Podesta (former Chief of Staff to President Clinton) talking to the group and it was at 8:30 in the morning and through the conference room glass I saw interns coming in and walking past and to this day I won't forget who they were. So it's important when you're at the internship to attend events and make an effort and appreciate that people are making time to talk to you.

Erin makes a very useful point on the importance of showing your appreciation for efforts made on your behalf. The other thing to remember is that if your sponsor or your university organizes a speaker or an event, you really should take full advantage because once you graduate and get a job, there aren't going to be lots of people setting up these incredibly valuable opportunities for you. Even if you're tired or you're busy, make the effort; if you never leave your desk and you can't be bothered to go anywhere after work you will have missed your chance to learn all you can about Washington and meet people who may be able to help you get your first job on the D.C. career ladder.

DON'T MAKE A BAD IMPRESSION

There is of course the possibility that, after going through all the trouble of finding this great internship, once you get there you are less than thrilled. It may have something to do with the internship itself and the kind of assignments you're getting, or there may be something else going on in your life that is distracting you. The other possibility is that you're really enjoying the Washington social scene and so you're less than 100 percent when faced with the prospect of being enthusiastic about anything at nine in the morning. Whatever the case, think hard about the message you are sending to your internship sponsors. "We had a girl last semester who seemed wonderful and dedicated at first but then started showing up late, then would just miss days and that sort of stuff; the fact that that happens just amazes me. So many kids want these opportunities. Not only is she basically wasting a spot someone else could have had but in this town everyone knows everyone and even if you don't know someone you ask two other people and they'll know them. So you're making an impression with everything you do" (Erin Green, Center for American Progress). Don't be shortsighted about this opportunity, and don't think people won't notice if you're not working to your fullest capacity. The people you meet and impress in this internship are the same people who can help you figure out your next career steps and can help you get there.

THE POWER OF NETWORKING

One of the most important lessons you can take away from this book is that Washington is a town of networkers and in order to succeed you need to be part of that. Liz Conroy makes the point very clearly:

> I have mentioned this to many interns; if you come out of this office and have not made at least three connections [with people] that you think you can ask . . . for help in the future, you are not doing your job networking. A lot of what your experience here has to be is an exercise in networking.

Every single one of us here got here because we met people in other places that have made a call—we made it happen. This doesn't just happen. Jobs don't happen through blanket resume submissions, it just doesn't happen that way. And I will help interns build those connections. One of our great interns this past fall is looking for a job and his legislative mentor has made countless calls, set up interviews for him.

Some students felt hesitant about asking people to talk to them about their careers or seek advice. While a little trepidation is understandable, particularly in a town like Washington where people seem to be very busy all the time, it is important to remember that networking really is part of the Washington culture. One student's experience is typical: "At my job they put all the interns through this leadership program and by the end of it I had a stack of business cards from people who I think were genuinely interested in helping me in my career. In Washington, everyone knows someone so just knowing a few people is so helpful." Chris Andresen also recognizes the interconnectedness of Washington and the need to use the resources around you: "It certainly doesn't hurt to come here and do an internship even if it doesn't lead to a full-time job with Dutko because when you intern here with someone you're basically getting access to their Rolodex and when you're ready to come back, that can be very valuable."

Take full advantage of all opportunities—speakers, lunches, events—even if it means working longer hours. Erin Green at the Center for American Progress offers this advice: "I send the students emails of the events going on in Washington and we really encourage them to take advantage of things. Of course you can't leave the office if you're really on a deadline but you really have to figure out those time management skills to take advantage of as much as you can. . . . You get jobs in Washington because of who you know. It's important to network not only with people here in the office but to reach out to other interns and other think tanks while you're here."

ATTENTION, SPORTS FANS!

Summer in Washington is, as we covered earlier, hot, muggy, and sticky. Despite this, a very large number of people get very excited about playing softball after work on one of the fields on the Mall. If you have any softball skills—and even if you don't—take advantage of this excellent networking opportunity!

Highlight of the summer? Softball. We have a softball team and we love for interns to play on the team and it's a great way for the interns to socialize with staff too. You could put those softball skills in a cover letter and it would help! (Liz Conroy, Senator Casey's office)

Softball. We used to be in the Senate softball league and now we're in a new league called the think tank softball league. So all the big think tanks are in it and all the interns are involved. It's a really good way for them to get to know other people—even if they're not playing they'll go to the game to hang out. I know it's a weird thing but that's a really important social part of Washington. And we'll go out with people from the other think tanks after the games—even the ones we're politically very different from—it's kind of funny. But interns should really take advantage of that. Whether it should help you or not, being the intern that hit the winning

home run might help you further down the road. Maybe they
don't know anything about your work product but they'll remember you and that helps. (Erin Green, Center for American Progress)

Try to get on a softball team. If you have softball skills, you
should definitely put that in your cover letter. That is all that
was talked about at work on the day of the game . . . and that
was a fun intern project, to leave work two hours early and
go stand on the field to reserve it. (college senior)

Networking is 24-7 in Washington; as this student describes,
your opportunities extend into many evenings if you do a good job
networking your workday away: "I think that networking in Washington is really important. I think there were some people in my
office who just networked all the time. They would really go out of
their way to meet people and engage people and I think they really
got a lot out of that. A lot of times our bosses would invite us to receptions and dinners and if you really take advantage of those kinds
of opportunities to go with your bosses to events, that can really
make a difference."

The other social thing in Washington, unfortunately, is happy
hour, so being underage can be a little tricky. I would certainly say
if you are under age and with staff from your office, you might not
want to put them in an awkward situation by drinking alcohol.

THE GREAT D.C. MERRY-GO-ROUND

In this section I am not going to talk to you about the actual merry-
go-round on the Mall (which is quite a nice merry-go-round), but
am using the term as a metaphor for the way people move through

jobs in D.C., often at dizzying speeds. Consider Michael Bassik's experience:

> You never know where you are going to wind up in D.C. even two years down the road. The person managing interns in Washington, D.C., is usually no more than two years older than the intern. And in a city where someone can move up the ladder so quickly, you never know when one day you'll be working with someone again. My former intern is now a client at a presidential campaign. Last year he worked in our firm learning how online advertising works for political candidates and now he is in charge of online political advertising for a presidential campaign and that's a one-year turnaround. . . . The intern coordinator who was at the White House when I was is now a client of ours at the DNC and I see him all the time.

The first implication of that is that obviously it makes sense to hold on to all those business cards you collected when you were busy networking, but more importantly to email them every six months or so just to be sure you don't lose track of them. As people move around Washington, someone who didn't seem like a particularly useful contact might suddenly become very, very useful, so keep in touch with everyone you establish a relationship with. The second implication reinforces what has been said elsewhere in this book: you might think you're a teeny fish in a teeming pond, which might make you think that what you do won't be noticed, but it really is a small town, so what you do, good or bad, will be remembered. And if it's a really good or bad story, it will be passed on. "You never know when you're going to interact with individuals again. Everything you do is going to be remembered. Really have respect for those you work for because one day they'll be your colleague and you want them to have respect for you as a hard worker, as someone who can be trusted; an internship is not an isolated event—it is really a tryout for a full time opportunity" (Michael Bassik).

TIPS ON LEAVING

On the last day of my internship it was funny I hadn't really felt like I was connecting with the people in the office apart from doing work and on the last day they all came around and gave me their business cards and said they would really be happy to help me connect to people and write letters and I was just so relieved. (college junior)

As you approach the end of your internship, you will be (or should be) thinking about what comes next. You'll probably have done a fabulous job and at some point you will want a letter of recommendation from your supervisor saying just that. I suggest you have them write the letter now, while they still remember who you are and can actually talk cogently about the work you did. You might also provide them with a list of projects you worked on, just to make it easier for them to be specific. Ask them to write a "to whom it may concern" letter, which you can then use for a number of different applications without having to go back to them each time to personalize. And if there is an application that needs a personalized letter of recommendation, they'll already have the text and can just add in who it's going to.

I would suggest asking your supervisor for the letter of recommendation about two weeks before you're set to leave, so that he can give it to you before you go. If, after ten days or so, you think he's forgotten about it, just mention it to him a few days before your last day and be sure he has your address. Of course, remember to send a thank-you note to the letter writer. Updating them on your job search provides you an opportunity to keep in touch. Once you get a position, that's another chance to email them and thank them for their help.

In addition to getting a letter of recommendation from your internship supervisor, you should consider getting letters (or asking if they would be willing to be a phone reference) from other people you did assignments for and even the person in charge of the office. One student was pleasantly surprised by an offer from her higher-up to help her in her job search: "If you just work really hard, that information will get back to the head honchos and even if you don't interact much with them, they'll come up to you at the end and offer to write you a recommendation if you need it because they know how hard you've worked and they really do appreciate your contribution" (college senior).

When you do leave, be sure to say goodbye and thank you in person (bringing in a sweet on the last day might be really welcome and appreciated—Washingtonians love free food), but also follow it up with a mailed (not emailed unless mail security is tight) letter of thanks that maybe summarizes what you liked best about the internship. Washington is a very small place, and you never know where your career will take you—it's smart to do the right thing, even if you weren't thrilled with your internship or you think your career will go in a totally different direction. One last thought on the leaving process: once you leave, you should check in with the person (or people) who you connected with best and who you've asked to be a reference. While you may have made a great impression and they would know you from a block away two years from now, remember that there is a lot of movement in Washington and lots of interns, and you don't want to be forgotten. "It's important to keep in touch.

If I have an intern this summer and then I don't hear from them for a year and then they want a job or a recommendation, it's hard to pull that together. But if they check in a few times over the course of the year, that will make asking for something much easier. . . . I get a lot of phone calls from former interns wanting jobs, wanting recommendations, and it's much easier to help them if you remember them" (Erin Green, Center for American Progress). If you're wondering what you could possibly email them about six months after leaving Washington, just a few lines reflecting on your D.C. experience and your ideas for the following summer would be fine. You don't necessarily have to ask for anything, though you should always say how much you value their advice. As you get closer to actually doing applications, you may email them again to ask for something more specific—a letter of recommendation, their thoughts on places you're applying to, someone they might know who might be willing to do an informational interview.

FINAL THOUGHTS

With this book my intent was to answer all of the questions I frequently get asked by students getting ready to go to Washington, and to offer some advice on making the most of the experience. Remember that this book is not your only resource; talk to friends, neighbors, professors, and your career services office. Washington is an exciting, vibrant place full of dedicated, enthusiastic people who are interested in how our government works and who want to be a part of it. You're likely to meet friends, mentors, and maybe even potential employers. I hope this book has prepared you for the experience—good luck and have fun!

WEBSITES MENTIONED

INDEX

ACKNOWLEDGMENTS

I am truly grateful to the internship sponsors and students who took the time to talk to me for this book. Our discussions helped me think about what was important to include in the book, and comments they made which are found throughout these chapters make this a better book than I ever could have written on my own.

ABOUT THE AUTHOR

Deirdre Martinez, Ph.D., is Director of Penn in Washington and a Lecturer at the University of Pennsylvania. Prior to earning her doctorate with distinction in education policy at the University of Pennsylvania in 2006, she worked as an advocate and policy analyst in the nonprofit sector and served as Legislative Director to Congressman Xavier Becerra (D-CA). Her dissertation, which won the Politics of Education Association's Outstanding Dissertation Award, adapts John Kindgon's multiple streams model to decision making within interest groups. Dr. Martinez teaches on the policy process and the politics of education, and her manuscript, "Hispanic Interest Groups in Washington," has been accepted for publication by SUNY Press. She also contributed a chapter entitled "Strange Bedfellows: Coalition Formation Among MSI Advocacy Organizations" to *Interdisciplinary Approaches to Understanding Minority Serving Institutions*, edited by M. Gasman, B. Baez, and C. Turner. She welcomes questions and comments and can be reached at d_martinez@sas.upenn.edu.